Project AIR FORCE

AIR FORCE COMPENSATION

CONSIDERING SOME OPTIONS FOR CHANGE

James Hosek
Beth Asch.

T0159556

Prepared for the
UNITED STATES AIR FORCE

RAND

The research reported here was sponsored by the United States Air Force under Contract F49642-01-C-0003. Further information may be obtained from the Strategic Planning Division, Directorate of Plans, Hq USAF.

Library of Congress Cataloging-in-Publication Data

Hosek, James R.
    Air Force compensation : considering some options for change / James Hosek,
Beth Asch.
      p. cm.
    Includes bibliographical references.
    "MR-1566-1."
    ISBN 0-8330-3187-2
    1. United States. Air Force—Pay, allowances, etc. I. Asch, Beth J. II. Title.

    UG943 .H67 2002
    358.4'14'0973—dc21

                           2002067969

RAND is a nonprofit institution that helps improve policy and decisionmaking through research and analysis. RAND® is a registered trademark. RAND's publications do not necessarily reflect the opinions or policies of its research sponsors.

Published 2002 by RAND
1700 Main Street, P.O. Box 2138, Santa Monica, CA 90407-2138
1200 South Hayes Street, Arlington, VA 22202-5050
201 North Craig Street, Suite 102, Pittsburgh, PA 15213-1516
RAND URL: http://www.rand.org/
To order RAND documents or to obtain additional information,
contact Distribution Services: Telephone: (310) 451-7002;
Fax: (310) 451-6915; Email: order@rand.org

In recent years, the Air Force has experienced recruiting difficulties as well as manning shortfalls in certain specialties. This situation has prompted the Air Force to consider significant alterations to the compensation system. The Air Force Chief of Staff asked Project AIR FORCE to provide an initial assessment of two alternatives under consideration, termed skill pay and capability pay. This report responds to that request. It draws on RAND's expertise in the area of defense manpower, where a persistent research theme has been to assess the compensation system's performance in terms of recruiting and retention. The report should be of interest to Air Force and other leaders with responsibility for shaping compensation and personnel management policies, and, more generally, to leaders and policymakers concerned with the relationship between the compensation system and personnel readiness. The research, completed in fall 2001, took place in Project AIR FORCE's Manpower, Personnel, and Training program.

PROJECT AIR FORCE

Project AIR FORCE, a division of RAND, is the Air Force federally funded research and development center (FFRDC) for studies and analyses. It provides the Air Force with independent analyses of policy alternatives affecting the development, employment, combat readiness, and support of current and future aerospace forces. Research is performed in four programs: Aerospace Force Development; Manpower, Personnel, and Training; Resource Management; and Strategy and Doctrine.

CONTENTS

FIGURES

TABLES

This document considers two possible changes to the Air Force compensation system: skill pay and capability pay. Skill pay is pay for designated skills, and capability pay is pay based on individual capability. The Air Force asked RAND to consider these pay concepts and bring to bear information on whether the Air Force should adopt them and in what form. To learn more about what role these pays might play, we reviewed the Air Force's manpower situation, considered underlying causes of problems, tracked relevant trends in civilian wages, and examined data on the level and composition of military compensation. With this information in mind, we identified possible changes in the current compensation system and addressed the potential benefits and implementation issues of introducing skill pay and capability pay instead.

INCREASED STRESS IN THE AIR FORCE PERSONNEL SYSTEM

The Air Force personnel system appears to have been under considerable stress. The percentage of "high-quality" recruits declined during the 1990s, as did first- and second-term retention rates and midcareer officer continuation rates—although first- and second-term retention rates improved from 1999 to 2000. In addition, during the latter part of the 1990s, the Air Force was less likely to keep its first-term high performers compared to its first-term lower performers. The same indications of personnel stress also occurred in the Army, but the Navy and Marine Corps showed either less adverse change or outright improvement during this period. The Navy and

Marine Corps were also more likely to retain their high performers relative to their lower performers.

Air Force personnel are increasingly called upon to participate in peacetime operations. The increase in the percentage of personnel who had any episode of deployment involving hostile duty rose during the post–Gulf War 1990s, as did the expected number of such episodes. However, we found that the increase in hostile episodes probably had little effect on first-term reenlistment.

COMPARING CIVILIAN AND MILITARY PAY

The supply of personnel to the Air Force, like that to the other services, has been affected by cyclical and long-term factors. The strong civilian economy hurt recruiting and retention. Low unemployment rates meant plentiful civilian job opportunities, and civilian wages grew steadily. The increase in civilian wages during the second half of the 1990s was faster than the increase in basic military pay. FY00 legislation called for basic pay raises half a percentage point larger than usual—i.e., larger than the increase in the Employment Cost Index. The scheduled raises, along with high enlistment and reenlistment bonus budgets, should help recruiting and retention, but the pay raises will not be fully implemented until 2006.

In addition to the fact that the civilian economy was at the top of the business cycle in the late 1990s, recruiting was affected by the long-term upward trend in college enrollment. This reduced the relative size of the traditional recruiting market and increased pressure on the services to improve recruitment from the college market. Another long-term trend was the faster pace of wage growth for persons with four or more years of college. Their wages grew unusually fast in the 1980s, and although this pace slowed in the 1990s, it was still faster than the wage growth of persons with only a high school diploma. The college wage trend encouraged college enrollment and created attractive civilian job opportunities for new college graduates and for military people with a college degree, especially officers. Looking to the future, it seems likely that civilian wages will remain high for college graduates, although the year-to-year increase in their wages might slow even more as the economy absorbs the increase in the supply. In addition, wage trends occurred in particular civilian labor markets: For example, wages rose rapidly for workers in information technology and employment opportunities were abundant for aircraft pilots.

Most of the difference in military pay among personnel at a given year of service is due to differences in rank and in pays and allowances related to location or circumstance; e.g., overseas cost of living allowance, Family Separation Allowance, and Hostile Fire Pay. When we compare the average pay over the career of Air Force personnel across broad occupational areas, the pay profiles are nearly identical. On average, the Air Force provides very similar career and pay opportunities within these occupational groupings. Within a grouping there is some variation in pay resulting from bonuses and special pays, yet these amounts are typically a small fraction of annual cash pay. This is not to overlook the large bonuses or special pays in certain occupational areas such as aviators, doctors, and nuclear-trained personnel that do in fact result in large pay differentials.

STRENGTHENING THE CURRENT SYSTEM

Given this background information, the Air Force may want to consider steps that could strengthen the current compensation system, in addition to considering skill pay and capability pay. We suggest four possible ways this could be done. First, the decline in Air Force recruiting and retention might have been lessened if more-timely and more-accurate information about civilian wages had been available. This information might have been useful in formulating budget requests, seeking a reprogramming of funds already appropriated to the Air Force, and developing more-precise information about the market forces that made recruiting and retention harder. We suggest the Air Force establish the capability to monitor civilian wages closely and with minimal lag. As part of this effort, it would be valuable to establish a capability to monitor the civilian wages of personnel who have left the Air Force. This should be done on a regular basis, e.g., as an annual survey of former members in their civilian jobs, with stratified sampling by specialty to assure sufficient sample sizes and with survey responses linked to members' service records.

Second, the basic pay table could be reshaped to make basic pay grow increasingly rapidly with respect to rank. Making the pay table more "skewed" toward higher pay for higher grades should cost-effectively increase retention, increase the incentive to exert effort and perform effectively, and encourage the retention of the most capable enlisted and officer personnel. Higher-percentage pay increases for middle and high-ranking personnel than for junior personnel would be a step in this direction.

Third, selective reenlistment bonuses could be restructured to make them worth more, with rewards more connected to skill level and grade level; and bonus budgets could be increased. In particular, anniversary bonus payments could depend on one's skill level and grade, which would create greater incentive to reach higher skill levels and be promoted faster. Tying bonuses to skill level requires a system that designates the particular "skills" and "skill levels" to be rewarded. The skill levels might or might not differ from the Air Force's skill level designator for enlisted personnel (i.e., 1, 3, 5, or 7).

Fourth, Hostile Fire Pay/Imminent Danger Pay could be revamped from its current form of $150 per month for any hostile duty or exposure to imminent danger during a month. The level of Hostile Fire Pay could be made to depend on the number of hostile episodes. Hostile Fire Pay for the current episode would be higher the greater the number of previous hostile episodes; personnel called on the most for hostile duty would be rewarded the most. This should help prevent lower reenlistment and could increase reenlistment among those who are called upon more often to perform this duty.

SKILL PAY AND CAPABILITY PAY

While we think the changes just suggested merit attention, they do not obviate the need to consider skill pay and capability pay.

Skill pay is intended to provide higher pay for certain skills. Presumably, the emphasis is on skill, not occupation; personnel with designated skills would receive skill pay regardless of their duty assignment and regardless of whether they used the skills in their assignment. It would be necessary to define "skills" and to establish a program to maintain skills and certify that they had been maintained. Skill pay would help conserve a *stock* of designated skills that are valuable for military capability and that might be costly and time-consuming to replace. These skills might also be in high demand in the private sector, although not necessarily. In contrast, bonuses help manage the *flow* of personnel in selected specialties in order to prevent current manning shortages due to such temporary factors as the business cycle. The personnel in those specialties might have varying levels of a skill. Compared with bonuses, skill pay has the advantage of being a more stable component of pay that would continue during a member's service career (or a designated portion of that career).

There are various ways to set skill pay. Skill pay might be a flat monthly amount or a percentage of basic pay with the percentage rising with rank, year of service, and perhaps time in grade. The skill pay table might designate a start point and an end point for skill pay, such as a certain year of service. The information system to help manage skill pay would presumably include data sources relevant to the Air Force's requirements for the skill; short- and long-run cost of replacing personnel with the skill, including the time to acquire the skill; and private-sector employment and earnings opportunities for those with the skill.

Special pays for aviators and physicians exemplify skill pay: The skill communities are well defined, have obvious civilian counterparts, and are costly to replace when shortages occur. In these cases, the occupational specialty and the notion of skill seem to overlap. In contrast, it seems less obvious which maintenance skills, administrative skills, or intelligence skills to include for skill pay. This suggests that each occupational specialty or skill area, however defined, would need to be handled on a case-by-case basis. Overarching criteria for the designation of skills that qualify for skill pay would then emerge through practice. Stability in a skill pay table, compared with year-to-year uncertainty, would also be advantageous. Special pays such as Sea Pay, Flight Pay, and Medical Officer Pay are revised infrequently and tend to be fixed additions to basic pay. If skill pay were set high enough, it would avert retention difficulties. But if skill pay were not regularly adjusted, it could become excessively costly if it is too high—and ineffective if it is too low.

Capability pay is intended to provide compensation and incentives for superior individual capability, especially current and prospective future leadership potential. The leadership potential could be for becoming a general officer; for heading a community such as acquisition, logistics, or intelligence; or for both. Capability pay has two potential advantages within the current compensation system. First, given the value associated with making military pay more skewed, capability pay could be designed to increase nonlinearly with rank. Personnel who qualified for capability pay would then face a pay table that in effect was more skewed. Second, the basic pay table and special or incentive pays are not presently designed to provide higher pay to more capable personnel, holding constant rank and year of service. Capability pay could do so. Skewed capability pay would therefore be expected to help retain the most capable personnel within a rank or year of service. It would encourage personnel to exert effort in order to qualify for capability pay and to reach higher levels of capability pay—which would not necessarily be tied to higher ranks. As a result, capability pay could help support a larger pool of highly capable candidates for the highest-ranking positions, compared with the current pay system. It would also provide personnel managers with more flexibility because they would have other ways to reward capability than through a promotion.

A capability pay system requires an accurate means of assessing performance to infer capability. A member's performance might be judged relative to the performance of peers, a set of standards, or both. To keep budget and administrative costs down, capability pay assessments of performance might not begin until, say, the eighth year of service for officers and until the rank of E-5 for enlisted members. The implementation of capability pay must be perceived as fair. Members should believe that the system gives all members an equal chance of being awarded capability pay, regardless of their assignment or occupational area. The award should be based on a member's performance as assessed by superiors.

If the system is perceived as fair, then capability pay can be paid to selected, high-performing members rather than to all members. For instance, supervisors could be told that only half the members under review could be recommended for capability pay. Even though the assessments would not be flawless, the repeated operation of the assessment process from year to year should work in favor of systematically identifying high performers. The current performance assessment system would presumably be used, but it would have to be adapted to map a given performance assessment to a capability pay award. Moreover, certification standards are being developed as part of the Development of Aerospace Leaders (DAL) program, and the attainment of DAL certification could be a factor in awarding capability pay.

Capability pay might be implemented as a smaller increment in pay over the remaining years of service, or as a larger increment over a shorter period. The level of pay could rise with rank, year of service, the level of capability pay already attained, or some combination. Including the level of capability pay already attained serves to multiply the rewards for high performance, thereby providing a strong incentive to excel at the beginning of a career.

Skill pay and capability pay may be helpful to the Air Force in both the short run and the long run, although more information and analysis are needed to determine the form, effects, and cost of these pays. Specific alternatives would need to be assessed in terms of the benefits and costs of alternative implementation strategies, their overall effects on recruiting and retention, their likely effects on pay levels relative to civilian pay, and their likely effects on incentives and on capability in different skill areas.

Alternative methods are available to analyze both proposals, including microsimulation modeling, experimentation, and survey methods. These approaches have been used successfully in the past to understand the effects on recruiting or retention of entirely new, "never-been-tried" personnel policies in the military.

In designing and considering alternative skill and capability pay proposals, it is important to recognize that long-term manning goals may be quite different from the goals of the past. The services are recognizing the advantages both of more-flexible career management across skill and occupational areas and of new methods of managing personnel, including greater use of lateral entry and outsourcing. These potential future changes imply that alternative proposals such as skill pay and capability pay deserve further consideration. Such proposals should be assessed using criteria that take into account the range of future Air Force manning requirements.

ACKNOWLEDGMENTS

We are grateful to Natalie Crawford, Vice President and Director of Project AIR FORCE, and S. Craig Moore, Director of PAF's Manpower, Personnel, and Training program, for their support and suggestions. We benefited from discussions with Col. James Wilkinson, Chief, Air Force Office of Compensation, and from material presented and discussed in the 9th Quadrennial Review of Military Compensation, where Col. Wilkinson serves on the QRMC Working Group. We also thank the Defense Manpower Data Center for providing data on military pay and personnel. We appreciate the efforts of our RAND colleagues Craig Martin, Mark Totten, and Jennifer Sharp in preparing computations and regression analyses, and Sydne Newberry, who improved the structure and clarity of the document. The quality of the report was substantially improved by the comments of our reviewers, Deborah Clay-Mendez of the Congressional Budget Office, Harry Thie of RAND, and Prof. John Warner of Clemson University.

AEF Air Expeditionary Force

AFQT Armed Forces Qualification Test

BAS Basic Allowance for Subsistence

BAH Basic Allowance for Housing

COLA Cost-of-living allowance

DAL Developing Aerospace Leaders [program]

DMDC Defense Manpower Data Center

ECI Employment Cost Index

FSA Family Separation Allowance

FY Fiscal year

HFP Hostile Fire Pay

NDAA National Defense Authorization Act

OCT Officer candidate training

ROTC Reserve Officer Training Corps

S&I special and incentive [pays]

SRB Selective Reenlistment Bonus

YOS Year of service

Chapter One

INTRODUCTION

During the late 1990s, the Air Force struggled with manpower supply problems. Recruiting failed to meet its numerical goal in FY99, and the proportion of high-quality recruits (high school diploma graduates with AFQT scores of 50 or above) fell every year from 1995 to 2000. Overall reenlistment rates frequently fell below their target rates, and reenlistment rates remained low in certain specialties. A number of factors have been proposed to explain these decreases: a booming economy with low unemployment, high private-sector pay for technically trained AF enlisted personnel and officers, and more frequent military deployments and hazardous duty assignments associated with peacetime military operations.

After 1999, the manpower supply situation improved. The Air Force increased its recruiting resources, Congress passed a multiyear increase in military pay in FY00, the economy softened, and an additional military pay increase took effect in FY02. Although the situation of the late 1990s is past, it has nevertheless stimulated discussion about the adequacy of the current military compensation system.

The purpose of this report is to provide information relevant to two compensation system changes under consideration within the Air Force: skill pay and capability pay. As we discuss in greater detail later, skill pay is intended to provide higher pay for certain skills, whereas capability pay is intended to provide compensation and incentives for superior individual capability. We also consider other changes that might be made to the current compensation system. Our approach is predicated on using empirical information about personnel outcomes to gain insight into the shortcomings of the current system. By appealing to empirical information, we can move from the abstract to the concrete.

Our approach is not limited to empirical information. The manning challenges of the past few years do not necessarily reflect the manning challenges of the future. Furthermore, important aspects of the compensation system's performance are not well captured by available data. For these reasons, past empirical information cannot be expected to cover the full spectrum of compensation effectiveness, and it is useful to have a conceptual perspective to delineate at least some of the additional aspects that should be considered.

As defense manpower research has progressed and the role of compensation as a strategic management tool has become better understood, the measures of personnel outcomes have broadened. In addition to meeting recruiting and retention targets, a compensation system should be judged on whether it retains high-caliber personnel and induces them to exert effort. It should assist in sorting personnel into positions of responsibility in accordance with their capability and productivity, and it should separate them when they are in excess supply relative to the organization's requirements. This document attempts to address at least some of these broader measures.

The Air Force requires a compensation system that can be relied upon to serve its objectives of providing national security through air and space power. The compensation system must be able to deliver an adequate supply of personnel to meet its manning requirements. The personnel must be highly selected, well trained, and highly motivated. The compensation system must be dynamically responsive and sufficiently flexible to respond rapidly and effectively when manpower shortages occur or loom on the horizon. Since the Air Force's capabilities in combat, combat support, peacetime operations, surveillance, mapping, intelligence, and so forth rely on its personnel, the compensation system must be viewed as a strategic management tool.

Yet the compensation system should support, not intrude upon, Air Force culture and the commitment of its personnel to accomplishing its objectives. It should operate automatically, be proactive rather than reactive, be predictable rather than uncertain, have low administrative cost, maintain cohesion (not promote divisive comparisons), be seen as fair, and be cost-effective. It cannot, however, be all of these things at once.

Changes in something as fundamental as the structure of compensation can also affect an organization's culture. Although it is difficult to place a value on culture—and often risky to challenge the status quo—it is nevertheless in an organization's best long-run interest to be open to even radical change. But although change may be feasible and may address certain problems, the prospective disruption to culture can still be forbidding. While we recognize the importance of culture, we have decided to focus on the actual and desired performance of a compensation system. Cultural considerations might be more productively assessed after we learn more about the improvements that skill pay and capability pay could produce.

A fact worth emphasizing: The military compensation system plays a critical role in determining the experience mix of the force. Compensation is naturally not the only factor that influences experience mix. In particular, each service constructs its own personnel management system and thereby specifies its own promotion policy. The Air Force differs from the other services in having higher reenlistment rates and slower promotions among its enlisted force. Air Force first-term reenlistment is several percentage points higher than that of the other services, but airmen reach E-5 about two years later than enlisted personnel in the other services. Still, given a service's promotion policy, the retention profile by year of service is strikingly similar across occupational specialties and fairly stable over time. Permanent changes in the level and rank/year of service structure of compensation can be expected to result in permanent changes to the retention profile and hence to the experience mix, all else being equal.

This fundamental fact makes it essential to know (or to question) whether today's experience mix is optimal, and further, whether it is optimal to have nearly identical retention profiles across all specialties. Whatever form the compensation system takes, it must be able to support the optimal mix of personnel. Additionally, if the Air Force wants the flexibility to change the experience mix within or between specialty areas, the compensation system must also be able to support such diversity. This report addresses whether the changes in the compensation structure suggested for discussion by the Air Force would permit such force flexibility.

In the 1980s and 1990s, the civilian economy changed in a way that increasingly rewarded, through higher earnings, those workers who were better skilled or had a college degree. The vastly improved economic opportunities for civilians with high-tech skills or with a college degree placed a burden on the services' efforts to meet their personnel requirements with high-quality personnel, especially in technical skills. The burden was particularly great for the Air Force, which relies heavily on personnel in information technology and with knowledge-based skills. Although the economic boom added to the burden, the competition for high-tech workers has also come from the information revolution and the greater value of knowledge (human capital) in economies that increasingly produce services rather than commodities and manufactured goods. The existence of better civilian opportunities for those with technical skills and higher education raises the question of whether there should be more differentiation in military pay to ensure that the best and brightest are retained, especially in key occupational areas and for future leadership positions. Skill pay and capability pay are ways of providing such differentiation.

Thus, at the conceptual level a host of issues must be considered. The most fundamental issue is the effectiveness of the compensation system in meeting recruiting and retention goals as the economy heats up and cools down. In addition, the compensation system must be able to attract, keep, and motivate high-quality personnel. It must also induce them to sort themselves efficiently, so that the personnel most capable of leadership actually stay and become the leaders. Similarly, the compensation system should provide personnel with exceptional technical expertise the incentive to enter positions where they can apply that expertise—and not be driven from service by a lack of professional growth opportunities or inadequate compensation incentives. The sorting and incentive roles of compensation are important because, lacking lateral entry, the services must recruit capable junior personnel in sufficient numbers at the entry level and then identify, train, and advance them to the top of the organization to become senior leaders and technical experts.

Another role of the compensation system is to assist in separating personnel in circumstances of excess supply, particularly at the end of their careers. These separations must be seen as fair even though they cut short promising and promised careers. The compensation system must adjust rapidly enough to keep pace with the private sector and have the capacity to reward different skills differently on a temporary or more permanent basis. The compensation system must be able to scale up (accommodate a large increase in end strength) in wartime and scale down in peacetime. Finally, although we focus on active-duty personnel, the compensation system for the reserves must be able to meet reserve-manning goals and do so without adversely drawing personnel away from the active components.

We review recruiting and retention outcomes in Chapter Two and private-sector wage trends in Chapter Three, also comparing military compensation across the services. This information documents the pattern of retention outcomes across occupations and the decline in the percentage of high-quality accessions. In addition, it helps identify underlying, causative factors such as civilian wage growth, low unemployment, college enrollment, and peacetime military operations—as well as the current structure of military compensation. Together, this information informs our discussion of the Air Force's late-1990s personnel situation and what steps might be taken to strengthen compensation and avoid future problems. In Chapter Four, we analyze a variety of options for improving the compensation system and consider the advantages and limitations of skill pay and capability pay in solving and preventing manning problems, relative to the current system. In Chapter Five, we conclude the report with a discussion of the importance of assuring sufficient flexibility in the compensation structure to meet alternative future manning requirements. We also point out the need for further assessment of skill pay and capability pay in regard to design (e.g., eligibility, amount, duration), effectiveness, and cost-effectiveness, in the event the Air Force or DoD decides to pursue these pay options.

Chapter Two

RECRUITING AND RETENTION IN THE LATE 1990s

We examined late-1990s trends in enlisted recruitment, retention, and reenlistment and officer retention in the Air Force compared with the other services to determine whether the Air Force faces personnel issues that differ in type and magnitude from those of the other services. We focused on the late 1990s because it is the period after the defense drawdown was completed and the end of Operation Desert Storm. Both the drawdown and the Gulf War caused aberrations in recruiting and retention trends (Asch, Hosek, et al., 2002). We also considered the effect of "perstempo" on reenlistment.[1] This examination of recent trends provides a backdrop for understanding the role that skill pay and capability pay might play in helping the Air Force achieve its manpower requirements and provides background for some of the reasons why these pays have been suggested as a means of improving manpower management.

RECRUITING HIGH-QUALITY PERSONNEL

During the boom, private-sector employment and educational opportunities were highly attractive to prospective high-quality recruits.[2] From 1995 to 2000, the Air Force and the Army suffered drops of more than 10 percentage points in the proportion of their enlisted recruits who were of high quality (Table 2.1). The Air Force

---

[1] *Perstempo* is the involvement of personnel in long or hostile duty.

[2] *High-quality recruits* are those with a high school diploma and a score in the upper half of the AFQT score distribution as normed in 1980.

Table 2.1

High-Quality Recruits as a Percentage of Non-Prior-Service
Recruits

	1995	1996	1997	1998	1999	2000
Air Force	82	81	77	77	75	72
Army	64	61	58	58	53	52
Navy	60	58	61	60	55	54
Marine Corps	62	62	62	62	61	60

SOURCE: Office of Accession Policy, OSD.

continued to lead the services in the percentage of high-quality recruits—72 percent in 2000—but this percentage had fallen from 82 percent in 1995. For all services, recruiting high-quality youth was more difficult than it had been a decade earlier. By the late 1990s, the increasing number of individuals who were college bound had depleted the high-quality recruiting population. In addition, private-sector wages had been rising steadily (see Chapter Three) and unemployment was extraordinarily low.

Within this broader context, additional reasons are needed to understand why the decline in high-quality accessions was smaller in the Navy and Marine Corps than in the Air Force and Army. Air Force and Army recruiting efforts seemed to be less effective than those of the Navy and Marine Corps, whose percentage point declines in high-quality recruits were less than half as large as those of the Air Force and Army. One study found that the effectiveness of Air Force recruiters declined in the 1990s relative to the 1980s (Murray and McDonald, 1999). Effectiveness is defined as the percentage increase in high-quality recruits associated with a 1 percent increase in recruiters, other factors held constant. Possible reasons for the decline in effectiveness include less (or less-effective) advertising; an inability to penetrate the college market; lack of sufficient recruiting resources (number of recruiters, recruiting stations, allocation of recruiters and stations to geographic areas); an inadequate level of enlistment bonuses and educational benefits; and less-than-fully-efficient recruiting operations, including recruiter management and recruiter performance incentives.

Generally, accession requirements for the Air Force and the other services grew in the late 1990s, whereas requirements were lower in the mid-1990s because of the defense drawdown. The Air Force's enlisted accession goals were 31,000 in FY95, 30,700 in FY96, 30,200 in FY97, 31,300 in FY98, 33,800 in FY99, 34,000 in FY00, and 34,600 in FY01.[3] It is possible that recruiting resources did not increase as fast as accession requirements did. From 1995 to 1999, the Air Force had between 950 and 1,050 production recruiters. This number increased to around 1,100 in FY00 and over 1,400 in FY01. The Air Force also made greater use of enlistment bonuses and spent more on recruit advertising in 1999 and later than it did in 1995–1998, but it may have taken a while for the advertising to have an effect on accessions.

External factors may have been equally responsible for the decreasing ability of the Air Force to attract high-quality recruits in the 1990s. The Air Force traditionally seeks recruits with strong technical aptitudes, but such prospective recruits were undoubtedly attracted by high-tech civilian job opportunities. Thus, even if Air Force recruiting had remained as effective as before, it might have been overpowered by the upsurge in high-tech civilian job opportunities. According to this hypothesis, which combines cyclical and long-term trend elements, labor demand declines when the economy cools off, thereby easing recruiting for all services. However, if the demand for high-aptitude skilled workers continues to grow, albeit more slowly, the Air Force recruiting environment will continue to be challenging. Offsetting these trends, to some degree, is growth in the population of youth ages 18 to 24, which is projected by the Bureau of the Census to increase until 2010.

RETENTION AND REENLISTMENT

The Air Force has been particularly concerned about retention declines at the first- and second-term reenlistment points. In this section, we focus on retention and reenlistment—the continuation of personnel at reenlistment decision points. We do not have separate information on the reenlistment or retention goals (or targets) of the

---

[3]Statement of Lt. Gen. Donald L. Peterson, Deputy Chief of Staff, Personnel, United States Air Force, to the Senate Committee on Armed Services, Subcommittee on Personnel, April 24, 2001. This is the source for our statements on accession goals, the number of Air Force recruiters, Air Force advertising, and (later in this chapter) first- and second-term reenlistment goals.

services, which together with continuation information would indicate whether the supply of personnel is adequate to meet the demand. However, the Air Force stated that it missed its first-term retention goals from the last quarter of FY98 until the second quarter of FY01, and second-term reenlistment also remained below goal at that point. Therefore, the downward trends in retention and reenlistment reported in the tables below appear to bear out that outcomes were below goal.

Retention rate is a commonly tracked indicator of enlisted retention. The Defense Manpower Data Center (DMDC) defines *retention rate* as the percentage of personnel who reenlist or extend, among those who reach a reenlistment or extension decision date within the 18-month period that begins at the start of the fiscal year. Extensions typically represent short obligations of additional service, often a year or less, whereas reenlistment reflects a longer commitment of service. We obtained first- and second-term retention rates from DMDC, and we also separately computed reenlistment rates for first-term personnel. We defined *reenlistment rate* as the percentage of personnel who make a new obligation of 25 months or more, relative to the population nearing the end of a service obligation and not extending. The service obligation could be either the end of a term of service or the end of a previous extension. *Extensions* are defined here as being 1 to 24 months long. (An Air Force reenlistment term is typically 48 months.)

From 1995 to 1999, the Air Force experienced the largest decline in first-term retention (Table 2.2) among the services: Its retention rate fell by five percentage points, or 12 percent. The Marine Corps' retention rate held steady, the Army's fell by two percentage points, and the Navy's actually increased. (The increase in Navy retention might have been related to its rising attrition rate, which would decrease the total pool of personnel who could choose to reenlist but would increase the proportion likely to reenlist. Thus, in spite of the Navy's increased retention rate, the net effect on the total Navy enlisted force could be a decrease.) In 2000, perhaps as a result of the pay increases contained in the FY00 National Defense Authorization Act (NDAA), first-term retention improved for the Air Force, Navy, and Marine Corps. The NDAA specified a 4.8 percent increase in basic pay, about half a percentage point above private-sector wage growth. The act also committed to higher-than-usual pay increases

Table 2.2

First-Term Retention Rates (%)

	1995	1996	1997	1998	1999	2000
Air Force	41.5	39.6	37.5	36.8	36.9	41.9
Army	40.2	38.7	41.8	39.6	38.2	38.3
Navy	33.5	37.4	36.2	36.3	38.6	43.5
Marine Corps	21.9	21.3	21.5	21.6	21.3	25.2

SOURCE: Tabulations provided by Defense Manpower Data Center.

through FY06, namely, basic pay increases equal to the increase in the Employment Cost Index (the usual standard) plus half a percentage point.[4] Service members followed the pay debate closely, judging from the many articles on pay in service newspapers such as the *Air Force Times*, and they were probably well aware of the strength of the FY00 pay action.

Reenlistment rates in the latter 1990s also fell. As Table 2.3 shows, the Air Force first-term reenlistment rate fell by more than did the retention rate. Between 1996 and 1999, the reenlistment rate dropped 17 percent—from 52 percent to 43 percent—with much of the change occurring in 1998–1999. Thus, a growing segment of those who were still enlisted a year after the end of their service commitment had obtained extensions rather than reenlisting. Part of this change may be due to random variation from year to year; e.g., 1999 may have been an unexpectedly poor year. Nevertheless, the 17

Table 2.3

First-Term Reenlistment Rates (%)

	1996	1997	1998	1999
Air Force	52	50	49	43
Army	41	48	45	43
Navy	32	31	35	33
Marine Corps	18	19	20	20

SOURCE: Authors' tabulations.

---

[4]The act also increased bonus ceilings, established a Thrift Savings Plan, and increased military retirement benefits for personnel entering service since August 1986, bringing their benefits to par with those of preceding entrants.

percent drop represents a large decline in actual reenlistments. (We do not have data on reenlistment rates for 2000.[5])

The Air Force also had the largest decline in second-term retention, where presumably most stay/leave decisions do not involve extensions. Its second-term retention rate fell from 61.7 percent to 51.2 percent, or 16 percent (Table 2.4). By comparison, the Army's second-term retention rate declined 7 percent (from 54.5 to 50.9 percent), and the Navy and Marine Corps rates improved from 1995 to 1997, then declined to their 1995 levels. The rates for 2000 show some evidence of improvement over 1999 for the Air Force, Navy, and Marine Corps.

Table 2.4

Second-Term Retention Rates (%)

	1995	1996	1997	1998	1999	2000
Air Force	61.7	58.9	54.5	50.7	51.2	52.0
Army	54.5	48.7	54.9	52.1	50.9	50.5
Navy	52.8	54.6	55.8	53.7	52.8	53.5
Marine Corps	41.4	46.1	45.3	44.9	42.8	44.6

SOURCE: Tabulations provided by Defense Manpower Data Center.

REENLISTMENT OF HIGH-APTITUDE HIGH PERFORMERS

Table 2.5 shows the first-term reenlistment rates for high-aptitude high performers and the remainder of personnel ("others"). *High-aptitude high performers* are personnel in AFQT Category I or II who had fast promotion times to E-4. In the Army, Navy, and Marine Corps, about 20 percent of those at the point of making a first-term reenlistment decision were high-aptitude high performers. In the Air Force, the figures were a bit higher: 24 percent in 1995–1996, declining to 20–21 percent in 1998–1999.

---

[5]Air Force data on reenlistment show a similar trend to that reported in Table 2.3. The Air Force excludes personnel deemed ineligible to reenlist, whereas the rates in Table 2.3 use data that do not indicate eligibility. The Air Force's first-term reenlistment rates declined steadily from about 63 percent in FY95 to about 50 percent in FY99, then rose to 52 percent in FY00. The Air Force's second-term reenlistment rates show a similar decline. Although our definition of reenlistment rate is not the same as the Air Force's, we find that the trends were nearly identical. Air Force rates are from Lt. Gen. Peterson's statement cited in footnote 3.

Table 2.5

**First-Term Reenlistment Rates for AFQT I-II Personnel
Who Were Fast to E-4 and Others (%)**

	1996	1997	1998	1999
Air Force				
AFQT I-II Fast to E-4	42	48	43	39
Others	55	51	50	44
Army				
AFQT I-II Fast to E-4	32	40	36	43
Others	43	51	47	43
Navy				
AFQT I-II Fast to E-4	37	35	34	36
Others	31	29	35	32
Marine Corps				
AFQT I-II Fast to E-4	25	26	26	24
Others	17	18	18	19

SOURCE: Authors' tabulations.

In the 1980 survey used for the purpose of norming the Armed Service Vocational Aptitude Battery to the civilian youth population, 7 percent were Cat I and 28 percent were Cat II. Although the comparison group's AFQT distribution may have changed somewhat since then, AFQT Cat I–II personnel score roughly in the top third of the youth population. Fast-to-E-4 personnel were in the fastest half of those who had reached E-4 by the time of their first-term reenlistment decision. Compared to their peers, they demonstrated a capability for higher performance in training, duty assignments, and physical fitness. Research under way at RAND suggests that high-aptitude high performers continue their high performance in subsequent terms of service, as witnessed by faster subsequent promotions. As a result, retaining such personnel is beneficial for military capability, for the capacity to train following cohorts of junior personnel, and for the supply of future leaders.

In the Air Force, the first-term reenlistment rate of high-aptitude high performers has been persistently lower than the rate for others (Table 2.5). This is not the case in the Marine Corps, where high-aptitude high performers were *more* likely to reenlist than others were, although the gap between their reenlistment rate and that of others has narrowed over time. The Marine Corps' comparatively higher reenlistment rate for high-aptitude high performers was probably supported by its low overall target reenlistment rate of around 20 percent: The low target rate allows the Corps to be highly selective—or rather it enables the Corps to induce high selectivity among personnel volunteering to reenlist.

The Air Force is certainly selective with respect to the quality of its recruits. For instance, in 1998 about 44 percent of Air Force recruits were Cat II, compared to about 33 percent in the other services. Furthermore, over time, the Air Force reenlistment rate fell by a greater amount among lower-quality personnel than among Cat I-II fast trackers. Therefore, even with a lower reenlistment rate among Cat I-II fast-trackers, Air Force reenlistees overall still include a high proportion of high-quality personnel compared to earlier periods and compared to the other services.

Similar to the Marine Corps, the Navy had *higher* reenlistment rates for high-aptitude high performers than for lower-quality personnel in 1996, 1997, and 1999, and the Navy's rates for both were nearly the same in 1998. The Army was more like the Air Force. In fact, the Army's high-aptitude high performer reenlistment rate was about 10 percentage points lower than the rate for others in 1996, 1997, and 1998. However, in 1999 the Army's rates were equal: The high-aptitude high performer rate rose while the rate for others fell. The Army's high-aptitude high performance reenlistment rate improved from 1998 to 1999, whereas that of the Air Force worsened.

If the definition of high-aptitude high performers is broadened to include AFQT Categories I-IIIA, a similar, though less stark, picture emerges. These data are presented in Appendix A.

INCREASES IN MILITARY PAY WOULD INCREASE REENLISTMENT

Retention responds to changes in basic pay and other forms of compensation, including reenlistment bonuses and retired pay. Estimates vary as to how a percentage change in relative military pay would affect first-term retention. A conservative estimate is that a 1 percent increase in the military/civilian pay ratio increases first-term retention by 0.5 to 1.5 percent. Using this standard in recent work, we estimated that declines in the military/civilian pay ratio and in the unemployment rate over the FY92 to FY99 period would have reduced retention by between 9 and 15 percent (Asch, Hosek, and Warner, 2001). Using a range of forecasts about future civilian pay and unemployment, we estimated that the FY00 pay action would go a long way toward reversing the 1990s decline in retention.

The FY00 first-term retention increase is consistent with this view. Still, shortages and retention problems may continue to plague particular areas such as aviation, information technology, and knowledge-based occupations. Therefore, the FY00 pay action, while it restructured the pay table to better reward promotion over longevity, did not necessarily address issues related to the need for pay differentiation across occupational areas. Neither did it address fundamental changes in the civilian opportunities that military personnel face. In the next chapter, we discuss these fundamental changes and the current degree of pay differentiation in the Air Force and other services.

THE EFFECT OF PERSTEMPO ON REENLISTMENT

Has the higher tempo of personnel use for peacetime operations hurt Air Force reenlistment? We find that although nonhostile and hostile episodes of deployment have increased, the increase has not led to a reduction in Air Force reenlistment. Reductions in Air Force reenlistment therefore do not appear to be the result of the increase in deployment episodes. This finding is conditional on the kind of deployments that occurred in the 1990s and on the deployment-related pays that members received. Future deployments might differ in character from those of the 1990s; by the same token, deployment-related pays could be adjusted in the future to help offset such negative aspects of deployment as combat danger, health risks, and separation from family and friends.

After the Cold War and Desert Shield/Desert Storm, military operations during peacetime emerged as a major component of national security strategy. The increase in peacetime operations has fundamentally changed the pace of activity for many military personnel, who must now support peacetime operations in addition to maintaining readiness for major theater war. The increase in peacetime operations was not initially recognized as a permanent change in the demands that would be placed upon the services—permanent in the sense that it would be a factor in defense planning in addition to major theater wars or large-scale contingencies. Yet during the 1990s, peacetime operations became commonplace as the services deployed personnel to peacemaking, peacekeeping, humanitarian, disaster-relief, and nation-building operations. In the late 1990s, the Air Force decided to reconfigure itself into Air Expeditionary Forces (AEFs), one purpose of which was to make deployment more predictable for airmen. Although the number and kind of deployments would not be more predictable, airmen would at least know whether their AEF was at the top of the list in case of a call-up.

We expect the increase in predictability to have a positive effect on morale and reenlistment but cannot analyze this with the available data. We can, however, analyze how episodes involving nonhostile or hostile duty affected reenlistment.[6]

Data on two special pays, Family Separation Allowance (FSA) and Hostile Fire Pay (HFP), allowed us to infer episodes of duty involving longer periods of separation and/or hostile duty. The receipt of HFP in a given month indicates hostile duty. The receipt of FSA in a given month indicates long duty (30 or more consecutive days) for personnel with dependents. Personnel without dependents are not eligible for FSA; we imputed long duty to personnel without dependents by referring first to the receipt of HFP in consecutive months and then to whether a majority of the service member's unit members with dependents received FSA, which indicates that the unit was deployed. The data therefore accurately record episodes of hostile duty for all personnel, with or without dependents. The data accurately record episodes of long duty for personnel with dependents. Because imputation is used for personnel without dependents, the data undercount episodes of long, nonhostile duty for these personnel, although the undercount appears to be small. Further, although FSA and HFP data are accurate and comparable across the services, they are not fully comprehensive. They do not count short trips from home station of less than 30 consecutive days, and they miss some longer episodes of nonhostile duty for personnel without dependents. (A more comprehensive database that captures "days away" is under development at DMDC.)

---

[6]This section is based on research under way at RAND by James Hosek and Mark Totten.

The involvement of personnel in long or hostile duty can be measured by counting the episodes of such duty over a period of time. Table 2.6 shows long or hostile duty rates for first-term personnel within a three-year window that covers the years before the date of a service member's decision to reenlist or leave.

The table indicates that the percentage of personnel with long or hostile duty rose in the late 1990s for the Air Force and the Army. In the Air Force, 39 percent of the personnel making a first-term reenlistment decision in 1996 had one or more episodes of long or hostile duty in the prior three years. By 1999, that figure had risen to 49 percent, an increase of 25 percent. The increase for Army personnel was similar, growing from 47 percent in 1996 to 60 percent in 1999, a gain of 28 percent. However, the percentage of Navy personnel with long or hostile duty in the prior three years declined from 69 percent in 1996 to 62 percent in 1997, then held steady around 60 percent. For Marines, the percentage held fairly steady near 75 percent.

As the percentage of personnel with *any* long or hostile duty rises, we expect to find increases in the percentage of personnel with *multiple episodes* of long or hostile duty. The effect on reenlistment depends on the precise pattern of increase in episodes. Specifically, an analysis of the relationship between long or hostile duty and Air Force first-term reenlistment implies that, compared to personnel without any episodes of long or hostile duty, personnel with long or hostile duty are in general *more likely* to reenlist.

We find that episodes involving no hostile duty have a positive effect on first-term reenlistment, and this effect is greater the greater the number of such episodes. Episodes involving hostile duty have little

Table 2.6

**Percentage of First-Term Personnel with Any
Long or Hostile Duty in Prior Three-Year Period**

	1996	1997	1998	1999	% Change, 1996–1999
Air Force	39	40	45	49	25
Army	47	55	58	60	28
Navy	69	62	60	61	−11
Marine Corps	73	77	77	76	5

SOURCE: Authors' tabulations.

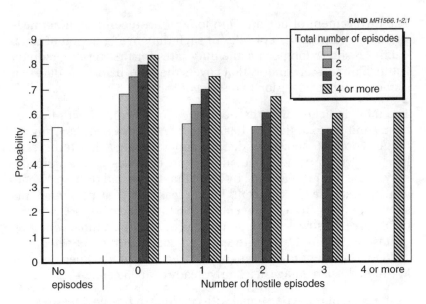

Figure 2.1—Effect of Episodes of Long or Hostile Duty on Probability of
First-Term Reenlistment

effect on first-term reenlistment, regardless of their number. Figure 2.1 is based on a regression analysis of the relationship between episodes of long or hostile duty and first-term reenlistment. The height of the bars in the figure indicates the probability of reenlistment for a point-of-reference airman with given characteristics. The bar at the far left is for an airman with no episodes of either long or hostile duty; the groups of bars to the right are for varying numbers of nonhostile episodes when there are zero, one, two, three, or four or more hostile episodes. Within any hostile-episode category, reenlistment rises as the number of other, nonhostile episodes rises. Looking at the leftmost bar in each group of bars, we see little change in the reenlistment probability for one, two, three, or four or more hostile episodes compared with no episodes. Again, hostile episodes had little effect on first-term reenlistment.

To quantify the effect on reenlistment of the change in episodes of duty between 1996 and 1999, we used the regression results to make predictions at the individual level. For example, according to the data, an increase in the percentage of personnel with any episode of duty (Table 2.6) should increase the percentage reenlisting. But among personnel with a nonhostile episode of duty, an increase in the number of hostile episodes should decrease the percentage reenlisting.

As shown in Table 2.6, the percentage of Air Force personnel with episodes of long or hostile duty in the three years prior to their reenlistment point rose from 39 percent in 1996 to 49 percent in 1999. Table 2.7 shows how the distribution of episodes changed between those years among personnel with episodes of long or hostile duty. More personnel had multiple episodes, and the increase in multiple episodes was driven by an increase in episodes involving hostile duty. The average number of episodes per person rose from 1.49 in 1996 to 1.67 in 1999, or 12 percent, while the average number of hostile episodes per person rose from .98 to 1.31, or 34 percent. Furthermore, although not shown in the table, 69 percent of personnel with episodes of either long or hostile duty had had a hostile episode in 1996; in 1999, this percentage had risen to 81 percent.

Table 2.8 illustrates the effect of the increase in long or hostile duty on first-term reenlistment. The table reports the predicted reenlistment probabilities for airmen at a given point in time (1996) who are assumed to have a given set of characteristics. With those factors held constant, only the change in duty episodes affects the reenlistment probability. In 1996, 61 percent of these airmen had no long or

Table 2.7

Episodes of Long or Hostile Duty in Prior Three-Year Period Among First-Term Air Force Personnel with Any Such Duty

		0	1	2	3	+	Average number of episodes
1996	All episodes		.65	.24	.07	.04	1.49
1999	All episodes		.56	.26	.11	.06	1.67
1996	Hostile episodes	.31	.48	.14	.04	.02	.98
1999	Hostile episodes	.19	.49	.20	.08	.05	1.31

SOURCE: Authors' tabulations.

Table 2.8

Effect of Long or Hostile Duty on First-Term Reenlistment

	Probability of zero episodes (%)	Probability of reenlist- ment given zero episodes (%)	Probability of positive episodes (%)	Probability of reenlist- ment given positive episodes (%)	Overall prob- ability of reenlist- ment[a] (%)
1996	61	55	39	61	57
1999	51	55	49	59	57

[a](Column 1 × column 2) + (column 3 × column 4).

hostile duty, and their reenlistment probability was 55 percent. The other 39 percent had long or hostile duty; given the mix and amount of such duty, their reenlistment probability was 61 percent. The overall reenlistment probability was 57 percent. In 1999, 51 percent of the airmen had had no long or hostile duty, and their reenlistment probability was again 55 percent. For the 49 percent who had such duty, the mix and amount of such duty implied a reenlistment probability of 59 percent. Thus, their reenlistment probability was lower than that of their counterparts in 1996. This is consistent with Figure 2.1, which implies that *among members with any episodes*, the average reenlistment rate will be lower the higher the fraction of those episodes that are hostile. But this rate will still be *higher* than the reenlistment rate among members with no episodes, whose fraction declines. Thus, the overall reenlistment probability for 1999 was still 57 percent, the same as for 1996.

These findings imply that we could hear complaints from some personnel whose nonhostile episodes were in effect turned into hostile episodes but still see little if any effect on overall reenlistment.

OFFICER CONTINUATION RATES

In this section, we review recent data on Air Force officer continuation rates and compare them to the rates for officers in the other services. As with their enlisted counterparts, officers' continuation rates in the Air Force have declined in recent years, especially for those in mid-career with 6 to 13 years of service; i.e., O-3s and O-4s.

On the other hand, continuation rates among senior officers, those with over 20 years of service, increased from 1994 to 1995 and then held fairly steady.[7]

Table 2.9 shows annual officer continuation rates since FY94 by years of service groupings. The continuation rate is defined as the fraction of individuals who were Air Force officers at the beginning of the fiscal year and were still Air Force officers at the end of the year. Year of service is defined as of the beginning of the fiscal year for each individual.

The table shows that the annual continuation rate has declined by more than 5 percent among those in mid-career. Although this decline may seem small, changes in the rates can accumulate over time if intervening actions are not taken. For example, based on the continuation rate of those in year of service (YOS) 0-5 in 1994 shown in Table 2.9, the likelihood that a new officer would still be in service by YOS 5 is $(.955 \times .955 \times .955 \times 955 \times .955) = .794$. Based on the rate for FY00, which is 1.7 percent smaller, the likelihood that a new officer is still in service by YOS 5 is .73, a figure 8 percent smaller than the FY94 figure. Thus, small changes in continuation rates can have noticeable effects over time, and moderate declines, such as those shown

Table 2.9

Air Force Officer Continuation Rates, All Commissioning Sources, by Fiscal Year (%)

Years of Service	1994	1995	1996	1997	1998	1999	2000	% Change 1994– 2000
0 to 5	95.5	95.9	94.7	94.0	94.3	93.7	93.9	−0.7
6 to 9	95.2	92.6	92.6	91.6	90.8	90.1	90.2	−5.3
10 to 13	95.6	92.1	94.1	93.9	91.8	90.1	90.6	−5.2
14 to 19	93.6	91.6	94.2	94.8	94.9	96.3	95.9	1.2
20 and above	69.7	77.3	77.6	76.7	78.2	80.1	77.5	11.1

SOURCE: Defense Manpower Data Center.

---

[7]This might be due to high-year-of-tenure rules being relaxed in 1995 after having being tightened during the drawdown.

in Table 2.9 for those in YOS 6–13, can have important ramifications for meeting manning requirements.[8]

To understand whether the annual continuation rates for midcareer officers in the Air Force are similar to the experience of the other services, Table 2.10 shows the annual continuation rates for YOS 6 to 9 for the other services. Continuation rates dropped for all the services between FY94 and FY00. But the Air Force experienced the largest decline in annual continuation rates for officers in YOS 6 to 9. The Navy experienced an increase in its officer continuation rate between FY94 and FY96, but the rate had dropped 3.1 percentage points by FY00. The Marine Corps and Army also experienced increases in their officer continuation rates between FY94 and FY97, but their rates declined thereafter. Although the Air Force had the largest drop in FY94, it is useful to recognize that the FY94 rate drop was the steepest of the period 1994–2000. Compared to the FY90 rate, the FY00 continuation rate actually represents an improvement over the decade.

The figures in Table 2.9 combine the rates for Air Force officers from all commissioning sources. However, the trends differ somewhat for

Table 2.10

Officer Continuation Rates, YOS 6 to 9, by Fiscal Year (%)

	1990	1994	1995	1996	1997	1998	1999	2000	% Change 1994– 2000
Air Force	89.6	95.2	92.6	92.6	91.6	90.8	90.1	90.2	–5.3
Army	91.6	89.6	90	91.2	91.8	89.7	89.6	89	–0.7
Navy	86.5	85.8	85	89.3	88.7	86.8	86	86.5	0.8
Marine Corps	88.5	87.8	88.2	89.9	91.1	90.4	90.2	90.0	2.5

SOURCE: Defense Manpower Data Center.

---

[8]Continuation rates must be combined with information on the inventory of personnel in order to project the number of personnel on hand in the future. An example of how small declines in continuation rates can have large effects on the experience mix of personnel if sustained for five years may be found in Asch, Hosek, and Warner (2001).

officers whose commissioning source was the Air Force Academy instead of other sources, such as ROTC, Officer Candidate Training (OCT), or direct appointment. Table 2.11 shows the trend in officer continuation rates for Air Force officers with YOS 0–5, YOS 6–9, and YOS 10–13 by commissioning source. The differences by commissioning source are important, as discussed below in the context of Table 2.12, because the occupational distribution differs by commissioning source. Consequently, differences in continuation rates by source can result in differences by occupational area.

During the initial commitment, from YOS 0 to 5, Academy graduates generally had the highest continuation rates, whereas direct appointments and those who entered through other sources had the lowest. A plausible reason for this is that the Academy group has a much higher percentage of pilots, who have a longer initial service commitment. Thus, at any point in time we would expect Academy graduates to have a higher 0–5 YOS continuation rate than officers from other sources. Yet over time Academy graduates may be subject

Table 2.11

Air Force Officer Continuation Rates, by Commissioning Source, by Fiscal Year (%)

Years of Service	1994	1995	1996	1997	1998	1999	2000	% Change 1994– 2000
0 to 5								
Academy	98.4	98.7	97.8	96.4	96.3	97.9	97.2	–1.2
ROTC	97.1	97.8	95.8	94.8	95.4	95	95.5	–1.6
OCT	97.7	98.5	98.2	96.4	96.1	96.9	96	1.7
Other	89.1	89	88.4	89.7	90	86.8	87.1	–2.2
6 to 9								
Academy	96.7	93.1	94.8	92.9	91.7	92.7	91.7	–5.2
ROTC	96.2	93.4	92.4	91.6	90.8	89.9	90.2	–6.2
OCT	96.7	93.9	93.9	94.2	90.5	91.8	93.0	–3.8
Other	89.8	88.6	89.3	88.2	89.9	86.3	86.8	–3.3
10 to 13								
Academy	97.4	93.7	96.1	94	88.5	85.3	85.8	–11.9
ROTC	95.4	91.1	93.2	94.2	93.2	91.1	91.4	–4.2
OCT	96.1	91.6	94.8	94.4	91	91.1	93.2	–3.0
Other	93.9	93.6	93	92.4	93.1	91.8	91.2	–2.9

SOURCE: Defense Manpower Data Center.

to the same external economic and internal force-shaping policies as officers from other sources. We see that continuation rates for those with 0–5 years of service have declined since FY94 regardless of source. For Academy graduates, continuation rates fell from a high of 98.7 percent in FY94 to a low of 96.3 percent in FY98. Continuation rates rebounded in FY98 and FY99, but did not regain the ground lost after FY94.

The annual continuation rates for those in YOS 6–9 also dropped steadily since FY94, with the largest drop being among those who entered the Air Force through the ROTC program. In FY94, the annual continuation rate for those entering via the ROTC program was 96.7 percent for those with 6 to 9 YOS (primarily O-3s). It fell to 90.2 percent in FY00. In FY00, those who had entered from ROTC represented 42 percent of all Air Force officers.

Among those in YOS 10–13, primarily O-4s, there was a precipitous drop in 1998 in the annual continuation rates of individuals who entered from the Air Force Academy. This probably resulted from the Academy having a higher proportion of pilots and a decision made in the early 1990s to extend the service commitment for pilot training to eight years after initial training, or a total of about ten years. (For the same reason, the YOS 0–5 and 6–9 continuation rates for Academy graduates were higher than they otherwise would have been.) Nevertheless, the annual continuation rate was 85.8 percent in FY00 versus 97.4 percent in FY94, a 12 percent drop. Because those entering from the Academy represent only 20 percent of all Air Force officers, the drop for all individuals in YOS 10–13 (Table 2.9) was smaller, 5.3 percent.

Table 2.12 shows the distribution of Air Force officers across 1-digit DoD occupational codes in FY99, by source of commissioning. Academy graduates are more likely to be General Officers and in Tactical Operations than are those who became officers through other programs. One reason for extending the initial pilot obligation was to keep pilots for longer periods while they were junior, which is where the bulk of the pilot force (tactical operations) are needed. Thus a 12 percent drop in the midcareer continuation rate for Academy graduates may impinge on the Air Force's ability to provide manpower to these areas.

Table 2.12

Percentage of Air Force Officers in 1-Digit DoD Occupational Areas, by Commissioning Sources, Fiscal Year 1999

Occupational Area	Academy	ROTC	Direct Appointment/ Other
1: General Officers	1.7	1.0	0.6
2: Tactical Operations	50.7	39.6	18.2
3: Intelligence	4.9	6.4	3.0
4: Engineering & Maintenance	12.6	18.6	11.2
5: Scientists & Professionals	5.0	5.3	8.6
6: Health Care	2.5	3.9	43.8
7: Administration	5.0	8.7	5.8
8: Supply/Procurement	7.8	11.0	6.8
9: Non-Occupational	9.9	5.6	2.1
Total	100.0	100.0	100.0

DISCUSSION

The Air Force manpower system appears to have been stressed. Symptoms include the decline in recruit quality, the decline in first- and second-term reenlistment (improving only recently), the higher loss rate for high performers, the increase in peacetime operations, and declines in officer continuation rates, especially midcareer (YOS 6–13).

The probable causes include both transitory and permanent changes: The economy had the longest period of expansion in the nation's history. The recruiting market changed fundamentally as a consequence of increased enrollment in two- and four-year colleges. For nearly two decades, the private sector sought and rewarded higher education, and the reality of higher pay for highly educated, high-ability people is likely to continue into the future. Peacetime operations have become a fixture of national security strategy, and during the late 1990s airmen were increasingly called upon for hostile missions. Why do these changes matter, and what do the changes imply for the military compensation system?

The decline in high-quality recruits is troublesome for two reasons. Research on enlisted personnel[9] indicates that in relatively complex tasks, individual and team performance in the first term of service depends on cognitive ability. Such tasks include the operation of Patriot air defense systems (Orvis, Childress, and Polich, 1992), multichannel communications equipment (Winkler, Fernandez, and Polich, 1992), and tanks (Daula and Smith, 1992). High-ability personnel perform better in these mission-essential tasks than lower-ability personnel, and high-ability personnel raise the performance of their team. Also, data from enlisted cohorts entering service in the 1980s indicate that the average AFQT of a cohort changes little as the cohort progresses through its military service life cycle. Both high-ability and low-ability personnel leave service, causing the average ability of those remaining in the cohort to stay about the same. Therefore, when cohorts of lower quality enter, they are likely to remain lower quality, and because they are lower quality their expected first-term performance is likely to be lower. Their later performance may also be lower, but we know of no research establishing that.

We identified a 17 percent decline in first-term reenlistment and second-term retention from 1995 to 1999. This was a serious loss of personnel for several reasons. The loss of early midcareer personnel after the second term reduces the capacity to train junior personnel and reduces the pool from which to draw future enlisted leaders. The loss of personnel after the first term exacerbates this problem because it means that the number of second-term personnel available for operations and training will remain relatively small over the next few years, and perhaps beyond. This makes it harder to arrange "work-arounds" in which personnel who are less than fully ready are advanced into positions otherwise filled by experienced second- or third-term personnel. The increase in first-term retention in 2000 is, of course, a welcome improvement.

The decline in first-term reenlistment was not neutral with respect to personnel quality. The Air Force tended to keep *relatively more* of its high-ability high performers compared to non-high-ability high

---

[9]We do not know of studies on officers.

performers. However, high-ability high performers had a lower reenlistment rate throughout the period 1996–1999.

We examined deployments and found large increases in the proportion of first-term personnel who had long or hostile duty at some point over a three-year period prior to their reenlistment decision date. The concern was that the increase in deployments had reduced reenlistment. We found a sizable increase over the late 1990s in the number of episodes involving hostile duty among personnel who had any long or hostile duty. Overall, we found that these changes appeared to have little influence on overall first-term reenlistment rates in 1999 vis-à-vis 1996. Reenlistment appears to increase as the number of nonhostile episodes increases and tends to remain unchanged as the number of hostile episodes increases. If the pace of peacetime operations remains at its late-1990s level, we can expect to see a continued higher incidence and greater number of hostile episodes for airmen, yet with little drop in overall reenlistment.

We also identified a roughly 5 percent decline in officer annual continuation rates among those in their midcareer. Although the amount seems small at first glance, even small declines in annual continuation rates can translate into dramatic declines in manpower over a several-year period. Therefore, this decline must be taken seriously.[10] Like the decline in retention rates for the enlisted force, a decline in officer continuation in midcareer represents a loss in the pool from which the Air Force draws its future leaders. We do not, however, have evidence indicating that this pool would become too small to satisfy the demand for future leaders. However, "workarounds" will involve promoting less-experienced personnel or imposing more duties on more-experienced leaders, thereby spreading them thinner across tasks. This could adversely affect Air Force capability.

---

[10]The extent of decline varies by area. According to Lt. Gen. Peterson's statement, the Air Force "has difficulty retaining officers with skills that are in high demand in the private sector" such as pilots, scientists, engineers, and communications and computer systems officers.

Chapter Three

A COMPARISON OF PRIVATE-SECTOR AND AIR FORCE PAY

From 1994 to 1999, civilian pay grew at a faster rate than did military basic pay. Although the year-to-year differences in military versus civilian pay growth over this period were not large, they accumulated, so that by 1999 enlisted pay had grown about 6 percent less than had civilian pay and officers' pay had grown 8 percent less. The relative decline in pay contributed to recruiting and retention difficulties (see, for instance, Asch, Hosek, and Warner, 2001).

Comparisons of civilian pay with military pay should distinguish between pay levels and pay trends. It will always be possible to find people in jobs that pay more or less than the military pays, controlling for age and education. Therefore, differences between military and civilian pay levels, even large differences, do not necessarily imply problems with the military compensation system. This is because pay is not the only factor influencing enlistment and reenlistment decisions. Other factors include the value of military training and experience and the individual's taste for military service—the latter a catch-all phrase for patriotism, pride, and other factors related to the preference for military service and the military lifestyle, such as a desire for new experiences, travel, and adventure. Furthermore, narrow measures of military pay can be misleading because they do not capture health care benefits, retirement benefits, housing, and other quality-of-life aspects. Nevertheless, as military pay declines relative to civilian pay, more people are disinclined to enter or stay in the military. Ideally, military pay levels are set high enough to attract and keep the quantity and quality of personnel required. To ensure that this will be so, military pay should be monitored over time relative to civilian pay and other harder-to-track items such as the value of military training versus civilian training, the pressure or intensity of work effort, the quality of housing, the level of health benefits, and so forth.

TRENDS IN PRIVATE-SECTOR PAY AND IMPLICATIONS FOR MILITARY PAY

Effects of Age and Education

Among civilian jobs, there can be persistent differences in wages by occupation. Much of the difference in wages across occupations relates to differences in age and education. Occupation accounts for a minor part of the variation.

Figures 3.1 and 3.2 present wage trends from 1995 through 2000 by wage percentile for age groups 22–26 and 27–31. Wages trends for age group 32–37 are similar to those for age group 27–31 and are not shown. The wages are self-reported weekly wages from the monthly outgoing rotation of the Current Population Survey. The wages have been deflated by the Consumer Price Index minus 1.1 percent, an adjustment for the upward bias in the CPI. Over this short period, the wage trends are similar under other adjustments—or even unadjusted, for that matter.

Figures 3.1 and 3.2 focus on civilian wage distribution by age and education. This is the range that military pay must be able to accommodate, including benefits, bonuses, special and incentive pays, and possible new pays.

Also, Figures 3.1 and 3.2 show wages for white males, which tend to be higher than those for women and minorities. Although our analysis (Hosek and Sharp, 2000) finds some differences in wage growth by race/ethnic group, the white male wage distributions are indicative of the overall wage distributions.

During the second half of the 1990s, the economy grew roughly 50 percent faster than in the previous two decades—increasing about 3 percent per year instead of 2 percent per year—and the unemployment rate fell to a 30-year low. Despite the vigor of the economic expansion, overall price and wage inflation remained moderate,

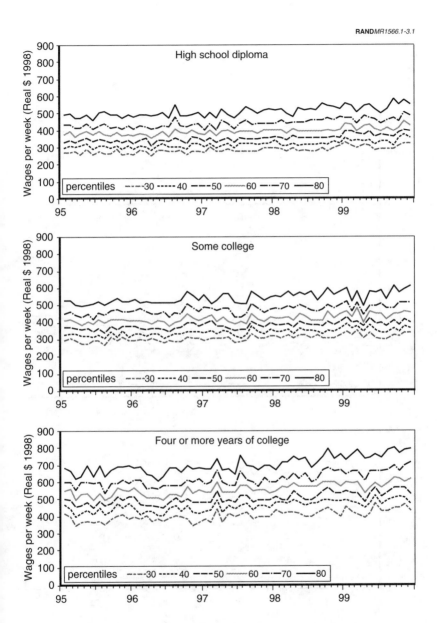

RANDMR1566.1-3.1

Figure 3.1—Wage Percentiles for 22- to 26-Year-Old White Males
with a High School Diploma, Some College, and Four or
More Years of College

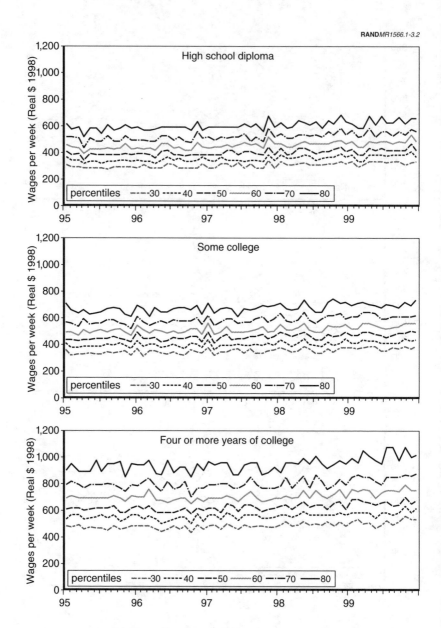

Figure 3.2—Wage Percentiles for 27- to 31-Year-Old White Males
with a High School Diploma, Some College, and Four or
More Years of College

and real wages (wages adjusted for price inflation) grew steadily. This was also true of wages for workers in the same age and education range as military personnel; i.e., full-time civilian workers in their twenties and early thirties with high school diplomas, some college, or four or more years of college. As an inspection of Figures 3.1 and 3.2 shows, wages are a few percent higher for workers with "some college" than for workers with only a high school diploma for any given percentile—the earnings differences between these education groups are not large. However, the wage gap between those with some college versus four or more years of college is substantial. This reflects the rapid growth in wages for college graduates during the 1980s, gains sustained in the 1990s. Further, the wage differences by education widen with age, as can be seen by comparing Figure 3.1 with Figure 3.2.

Implications of Wage Trends for the Air Force

The three educational strata shown in Figures 3.1 and 3.2 are relevant to Air Force personnel. Virtually every Air Force recruit has a high school diploma, and a small percentage of recruits have some college. Since the Air Force is highly selective in recruiting, the upper half of the high school wage distribution is more relevant than the lower half. Also, since Air Force recruits often score in the upper half of the AFQT score distribution and high scorers are more likely to seek higher education, the some-college and full-college wage distributions are relevant. Most Air Force enlistees add to their education while in service, so by the end of the first term the majority of enlistees have some college. It is reasonable to compare their military pay to the civilian pay of workers with some college. Also, most enlistees sign up for educational benefits, which can be understood as an expression of interest in keeping open the option for further higher education. The high wages received by workers with baccalaureate degrees are of course a stimulus for persons with high school or some college to complete four or more years of college.

The Air Force has been foremost among the services in emphasizing the value of education and facilitating its acquisition in the service. The Air Force and its members realize the importance of education and training in building the skills needed for superior military capability. The Air Force has a reputation for providing excellent training, and the skills and knowledge learned are often highly transferable to the civilian world. Indeed, when comparing military and civilian pay, the value of training should not be overlooked. In cases where skills are transferable and the organization is paying the costs of training and education, pay can be lower during training years if it is anticipated to be higher later. After the training period, however, pay must be increased to keep more of the people trained. For instance, the Air Force trains aircraft mechanics and electronic equipment repairers. Air Force pay may be lower in the early career than private-sector pay for these occupations, yet during the formative years of training the lower pay is offset by the expectation of higher future earnings and better job opportunities in the Air Force, the private sector, or both.

During the economic expansion, employers may have been more willing to offer training, subsidize education, and pay higher wages to junior employees making their way up the learning curve. According to this hypothesis (as suggested in Chapter Two), the Air Force was simply outcompeted in its tight labor market niche by civilian firms.

The time period shown in Figures 3.1 and 3.2, 1995–2000, was a period of unusually strong economic growth. But the growing gap between college wages and high school wages has been a long-term trend, not a by-product of the strong economy. Given the Air Force emphasis on skill attainment and college education even among the enlisted force, this fundamental change in the civilian wage structure is highly relevant to the Air Force. As discussed in a paper for the 9th Quadrennial Review of Military Compensation, the change argues for a relatively higher military pay increase for midcareer and senior enlisted members, many of whom have attained some college (Asch, Hosek, and Warner, 2001).

THE CURRENT AIR FORCE COMPENSATION SYSTEM

The current military compensation system provides authorities for many special and incentive pays and allowances to tailor compensation to the services' needs. Research under way at RAND suggests that the incidence and average amounts of these pays and allowances differ across services and occupational areas. But the differences are overshadowed by similarities in the average amounts of the components of Regular Military Compensation (RMC): basic pay, subsistence allowance, housing allowance, and the tax advantage stemming from the nontaxability of these allowances.

Because RMC is so similar for a given YOS and is the principal determinant of total pay, average pay is fairly similar for individuals at a given YOS, regardless of branch or service or broad occupational area. Put differently, pay differences at a given YOS are relatively small. In contrast, average pay for Air Force enlisted personnel is about 5 percent less than it is for the other branches of service, reflecting the slower promotion rates to E5 and E6.[1] Average pay for Air Force officers whose commissioning source was ROTC or the Academy stands relatively comparable to the pay of officers in the other branches of service.

Table 3.1 shows the incidence and the average amount (among those who received it) of most components of current military pay for enlisted personnel in 1999. Table 3.2 is a similar table for officers whose source of commissioning was either a military academy or ROTC. The averages are taken for those individuals who were on active duty for the full calendar year of 1999 and are based on actual monthly pay data for that year. Care is needed in interpreting the enlistment and SRB figures because the averages in Tables 3.1 and 3.2 confound initial payment of the bonus, which may be large, with smaller anniversary payments. As these tables make clear, in 1999 the incidence and average amounts of special and incentive pays and of allowances varied considerably across the branches of service. As expected, Career Sea Pay is pervasive in the Navy. About 40 percent of Navy enlisted personnel and about 19 percent of Navy officers received either Career Sea Pay or Career Sea Pay Premiums. Among enlisted personnel, no other special and incentive pay is as dominant as Sea Pay. Among Air Force enlisted personnel, Foreign Duty Pay covered

---

[1]We mentioned in Chapter One that promotions to E-5 occur at a later year of service and reenlistment rates are typically higher in the Air Force than in the other services. It is worth mentioning here that Congress places constraints on the percentage of personnel in grades E-5 through E-9. It is possible that these constraints are a factor in the slower promotion to E-5. If so, increasing the allowable E-5-to-E-9 percentage would permit faster promotion to E-5. We have not analyzed this possibility. Faster promotion would in effect increase military pay. Also, if more personnel were in E-5, the required personnel budget would increase

Table 3.1
Incidence and Average Amounts of Enlisted Pay, 1999

Type of pay	Army % Receiving	Army Average Amount	Air Force % Receiving	Air Force Average Amount	Marine Corps % Receiving	Marine Corps Average Amount	Navy % Receiving	Navy Average Amount
Basic Pay	100.0	$19,542	100.0	$20,371	100.0	$17,611	100.0	$19,757
BAH (Green Book)	100.0	$6,497	100.0	$6,559	100.0	$6,245	100.0	$6,453
BAS (Green Book)	100.0	$2,738	100.0	$2,738	100.0	$2,738	100.0	$2,738
Tax advantage (Green Book)	100.0	$1,732	100.0	$1,731	100.0	$1,647	100.0	$1,707
Average RMC		**$30,509**		**$31,398**		**$28,241**		**$30,655**
Foreign Duty Pay	28.1	$73	25.2	$65	10.3	$35	5.3	$90
Proficiency Pay	6.1	$2,699	3.0	$2,285	5.8	$2,583	9.4	$2,108
Oversea Extension Pay	0.4	$696	0.1	$434	1.5	$1,212	0.4	$675
Career Sea Pay	0.1	$1,314	0.0	$112	9.0	$205	40.5	$1,624
Career Sea Pay Premium	0.0	$742	0.0		0.0	$734	5.1	$684
Hostile Fire Pay	15.7	$633	19.8	$570	12.1	$468	26.1	$511
Diving Duty Pay	0.1	$1,744	0.3	$1,687	0.3	$1,800	1.7	$2,007
Submarine Duty Pay	0.0		0.0		0.0		7.5	$2,094
Foreign Language Pay (1)	1.5	$675	1.5	$806	0.7	$620	0.5	$715
Foreign Language Pay (2)	0.2	$332	0.1	$360	0.0		0.0	$373
Flying Pay (crew member)	1.0	$1,688	3.1	$1,979	1.3	$1,847	1.9	$2,120

Table 3.1 (continued)

Type of pay	Army		Air Force		Marine Corps		Navy	
	% Receiving	Average Amount	% Receiving	Average Amount	% Receiving	Average Amount	% Receiving	Average Amount
Flying Pay (noncrew member)	0.0		0.0		0.8	$1,003	0.0	
Parachute Duty Pay	10.1	$1,471	0.2	$1,078	0.7	$1,095	0.3	$1,417
Flight Deck Duty Pay	0.0	$1,200	0.0	$85	2.4	$471	9.0	$591
Demolition Duty Pay	0.4	$1,567	0.4	$1,641	0.3	$1,475	0.5	$1,406
Experiment Stress Duty Pay	0.0	$870	0.2	$1,261	0.0	$1,387	0.2	$747
Toxic Fuels Duty Pay	0.0	$261	0.3	$1,507	0.0		0.0	$303
Toxic Pesticides Duty	0.0	$532	0.0	$1,166	0.0		0.0	$998
High Altitude Low Opening Pay	0.3	$2,297	0.3	$2,399	0.2	$2,207	0.5	$2,498
Chemical Munitions Duty Pay	0.1	$927	0.0	$813	0.0		0.0	$546
Average S&I Pay		**$482**		**$301**		**$317**		**$1,345**
Family Separation Allowance I	1.4	$181	0.7	$308	0.0		0.8	$180
Family Separation Allowance II	19.9	$417	17.1	$333	19.2	$385	23.0	$399
CONUS COLA	0.6	$730	0.6	$355	1.4	$612	0.7	$697
Oversea COLA	24.6	$1,849	24.1	$2,904	21.4	$2,240	19.4	$2,748
Clothing/Uniform Allowance	87.2	$329	90.8	$281	97.9	$229	99.7	$336

Table 3.1 (continued)

Type of pay	Army		Air Force		Marine Corps		Navy	
	% Receiving	Average Amount	% Receiving	Average Amount	% Receiving	Average Amount	% Receiving	Average Amount
Average miscellaneous allowances/COLAs		$832		$1,015		$785		967
Enlistment Bonus	3.0	$5,193	1.7	$3,749	0.5	$2,137	2.2	$4,139
SRB	11.2	$1,949	10.1	$3,167	0.0		15.4	$4,452
Average bonus		$372		$381		$11		$777

SOURCE: Asch, Hosek, and Martin (forthcoming).

Table 3.2

Incidence and Average Amounts of Officer Pay, 1999
(Commissioning Source Is ROTC or a Military Academy)

Type of Pay	Army % Receiving	Army Average Amount	Air Force % Receiving	Air Force Average Amount	Marine Corps % Receiving	Marine Corps Average Amount	Navy % Receiving	Navy Average Amount
Basic Pay	100.0	$45,322	100.0	$45,127	100.0	$42,675	100.0	$43,558
BAH (Green Book)	100.0	$10,584	100.0	$10,683	100.0	$10,522	100.0	$10,376
BAS (Green Book)	100.0	$1,887	100.0	$1,887	100.0	$1,887	100.0	$1,887
Tax advantage (Green Book)	100.0	$3,896	100.0	$3,902	100.0	$3,623	100.0	$3,939
Average RMC		**$61,689**		**$61,599**		**$58,707**		**$59,761**
Saved Pay	0.0		0.0		0.0		0.0	$4,248
Health Professional Saved Pay	0.0		0.0		0.0		0.0	
Variable Special Pay	0.3	$8,141	0.1	$8,517	0.0		0.0	$8,751
Board Certified Pay	1.8	$3,236	1.0	$3,435	0.0		0.4	$3,656
Aviation Career Incentive Pay	9.4	$5,917	41.8	$6,155	33.0	$5,370	38.5	$5,456
Responsibility Pay	0.0		0.0		0.0		0.0	
Career Sea Pay	0.0		0.0	$150	0.2	$418	18.9	$1,272
Career Sea Pay Premium	0.0		0.0	$67	0.0		3.8	$544
Hostile Fire Pay	17.6	$621	21.8	$576	15.5	$474	24.8	$525
Diving Duty Pay	0.1	$1,599	0.1	$1,682	0.5	$1,650	2.8	$2,249
Submarine Duty Pay	0.0		0.0		0.0		9.9	$5,004
Foreign Language Pay (1)	3.1	$730	2.6	$915	1.4	$802	0.8	$739

Table 3.2—continued

Type of Pay	Army		Air Force		Marine Corps		Navy	
	% Receiving	Average Amount	% Receiving	Average Amount	% Receiving	Average Amount	% Receiving	Average Amount
Foreign Language Pay (2)	0.4	$349	0.1	$321	.0		0.0	$400
Flying Pay (Crew member)	0.1	$1,735	0.8	$1,551	0.0		0.1	$1,722
Flying Pay (noncrew member)	0.1	$1,047	0.1	$604	0.1	$774	0.1	$728
Air Weapons Controller (crew)	0.0	$2,028	1.0	$2,564	0.0		0.0	$2,400
Parachute Duty Pay	11.2	$1,264	0.2	$1,019	1.6	$1,057	0.6	$1,421
Flight Deck Duty Pay	0.0		0.0		0.2	$558	4.8	$485
Demolition Duty Pay	0.3	$1,413	0.1	$1,374	0.1	$547	0.8	$1,360
Experimental Stress Duty Pay	0.0	$1,028	0.3	$1,049	0.0		0.1	$785
Toxic Fuels Duty Pay	0.0		0.1	$1,438	0.0		0.0	
High Altitude Low Opening Pay						$2,700		
Chemical Munitions Duty Pay	0.2	$1,981	0.2	$2,181	0.0		0.7	$2,504
	0.0	$964	0.0		0.0		0.0	
Average S&I pay		**$927**		**$2,810**		**$1,889**		**$3,134**
FSA I	1.3	$520	0.6	$603	0.0		0.7	$189
FSA II	15.2	$387	14.5	$306	18.3	$346	21.5	$380
CONUS COLA	1.2	$985	1.9	$439	1.6	$1,007	1.2	$1,070
Overseas COLA	23.2	$3,243	16.7	$4,300	14.5	$4,996	17.6	$4,391

Table 3.2—continued

Type of Pay	Army		Air Force		Marine Corps		Navy	
	% Receiving	Average Amount	% Receiving	Average Amount	% Receiving	Average Amount	% Receiving	Average Amount
Clothing/uniform allowance	1.3	$529	0.8	$575	1.2	$371	1.3	$384
Personal Money Allowance	0.0	$843	0.0	$321	0.0		0.0	$497
Average miscellaneous allowances/COLAs		$837		$779		$810		$872
Nuclear Officer Accession Bonus	0.0		0.0		0.0		0.0	$7,000
Medical Officer Retention Bonus	0.8	$36,260	0.4	$35,355	0.0		0.2	$36,576
Nuclear Career Accession Bonus	0.0		0.0		0.0		1.2	$2,039
Nuclear Career Annual Incentive Bonus	0.0		0.0		0.0		2.5	$7,402
Additional Special Pay, Medical Officer	2.0	$14,729	1.1	$15,000	0.0	$42	0.6	$14,707

Table 3.2—continued

Type of Pay	Army % Receiving	Army Average Amount	Air Force % Receiving	Air Force Average Amount	Marine Corps % Receiving	Marine Corps Average Amount	Navy % Receiving	Navy Average Amount
Incentive Special Pay, Medical Officer	0.4	$20,852	0.3	$18,304	0.0		0.1	$22,195
Nuclear Qualified Officer Continuation	0.0		0.0		0.0		5.5	$17,435
Aviation Officer Continuation	0.0		7.6	$17,657	6.8	$11,136	6.7	$12,163
Average bonuses		$673		$1,695		$756		$2,172
Average annual pay		**$64,125**		**$66,883**		**$62,161**		**$65,940**

SOURCE: Asch, Hosek, and Martin (forthcoming).

about a quarter of individuals in 1999, and Hostile Fire Pay covered about a fifth of the individuals. But these pays were also pervasive in the Army and to some extent in the Marine Corps. A few pays, such as Flying Pay, benefit the Air Force much as Sea Pay benefits the Navy personnel, but relatively few enlisted personnel receive them. For instance, only 3.1 percent of enlisted personnel received Flying Pay in 1999.

Among officers whose commissioning source was an academy or ROTC, special and incentive pays and allowances varied across service branch as well (Table 3.2). The dollar amounts of special and incentive pays for medical officers were particularly high. For Air Force officers, Aviator Career Incentive Pay was among the most prevalent special and incentive (S&I) pays, covering about 42 percent of officers commissioned from ROTC or an academy. This source of pay was also prevalent among Marine Corps and Navy officers. However, the average dollar amount was somewhat higher in the Air Force. The incidence and average dollar amount of aviation officer continuation pay was also higher in the Air Force, although it only covered 7.6 percent of officers in 1999.

Enlistment Bonuses

Table 3.3 shows the incidence and average amounts of first payments and anniversary payments of enlistment and reenlistment bonuses by service. The Air Force has increased its use of enlistment and reenlistment bonuses in recent years. In FY00 the Selective Reenlistment Bonus (SRB) budget was doubled relative to FY99—from $60 million to $120 million—and the percentage of occupational specialties covered by selective reenlistment bonuses rose from 57 to 73 percent. The figures in Tables 3.1 and 3.3 for enlisted personnel provide a baseline of how many individuals were covered by bonuses in 1999 and how the figures differ in the Air Force relative to the other services.

About 10 percent of all Air Force enlisted personnel received an SRB payment in 1999. Since bonus payments may be spread out over several years, this figure includes both those receiving a bonus for the first time and those receiving an anniversary payment. Among

Table 3.3

Incidence and Average Amount of Enlistment and Selective Reenlistment Bonuses, 1999

Bonus Incidence and Amount	Army	Air Force	Marine Corps	Navy
Enlistment bonuses				
Percent receiving first payment[a]	2.1%	1.7%	0.5%	1.9%
Average first payment	$5,249	$3,744	$2,137	$4,321
First payment as percentage of basic pay	40.1%	29.2%		1.3%
Percent receiving anniversary payment[a]	01.7%	0.0%	0.0%	0.7%
Average anniversary payment	$2,312	$1,200	.	$982
Anniversary payment as percentage of basic pay	017.4%	09.3%	.	06.6%
SRBs				
Percent receiving first payment[a]	3.7%	4.3%	0.0%	4.0%
Average first payment	$3,424	$5,672	.	$8,973
First payment as percentage of basic pay	19.4%	32.8%	.	51.3%
Percent receiving anniversary payment[a]	7.8%	6.0%	0.0%	14.2%
Average anniversary payment	$1,060	$1,293	.	$2,388
Anniversary payment as percentage of basic pay	.4%	6.7%	.	12.1%

[a]Percentages are computed relative to the total number of personnel in service all 12 months of 1999. For first-year personnel, the sample includes personnel who entered service in October–December 1998, plus those entering in January 1999, and who stayed in service throughout 1999. Because first payments of enlistment bonuses are received upon entering service but the sample contains only four months worth of entrants (October–January), the sample undercounts the percentage of personnel receiving first payments of enlistment bonuses. Allowing for entrants throughout the year would approximately triple the percentage.

Air Force enlisted personnel, 4.3 percent received payments for the first time and 6.0 percent received anniversary payments (for a total of about 10 percent). The average dollar amount for first-time payments was $5,672, a figure less than the Navy's average first-time SRB payment but more than the Army's. Air Force personnel were also less likely to get an enlistment bonus, and the average dollar amount was smaller relative to that of the Army or Navy.

Average Total Pay

Despite the differences across the services in S&I pays and allowances shown in the tables, average total pay is fairly similar across the branches of service, for a given year of service. Figure 3.3 shows average enlisted pay by year of service, broken out by category: basic pay, Basic Allowance for Housing (BAH), Basic Allowance for Subsistence (BAS), federal tax advantage, special and incentive pays, bonuses, miscellaneous allowances, and cost-of-living allowances (COLAs). Figure 3.4 shows the averages for officers whose

RAND*MR1566.1-3.3*

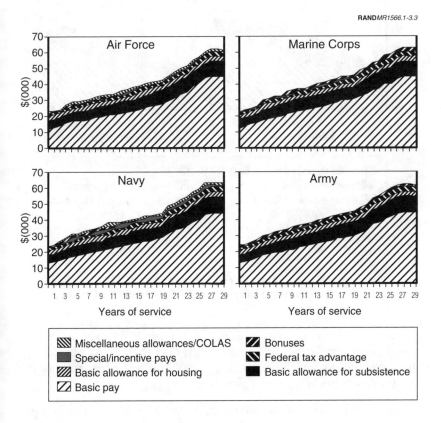

Figure 3.3—Average Total Enlisted Pay by Years of Service, 1999

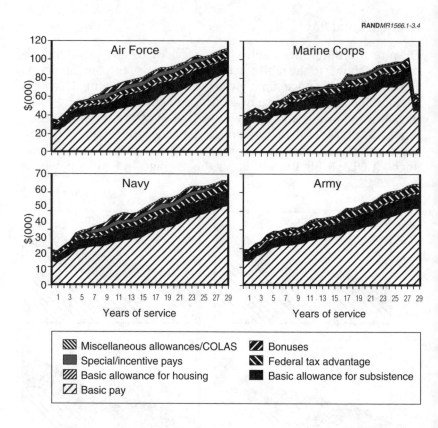

RAND*MR1566.1-3.4*

Figure 3.4—Average Officer Pay by Years of Service (Commissioning Source Is Academy or ROTC), 1999

source of commission was either ROTC or a military academy. Despite the similarities, the small differences that do exist in average total pay often favor the Navy, Army, and Marine Corps, and not the Air Force—especially in the case of enlisted pay.

When all categories of pay are included, average annual enlisted pay for a new recruit in YOS 1 is about $23,000, as shown in Figure 3.3. By YOS 10, average annual pay has grown to about $33,000. By YOS 20, average total enlisted pay is about $42,000. Average annual pay grows steeply after 20 YOS because enlisted personnel in lower grades retire at 20, and those who remain are a highly selected group of senior enlisted personnel in the higher grades, particularly E-8 and E-9. Although average pay varies by YOS, it does not vary much across services for a given YOS for the Army, Navy, and Marine Corps. At YOS 10, average total pay is $35,007 for the Army, $35,675 for the Marine Corps and $35,863 for the Navy. The Air Force's figure of $33,621 reflects slower promotion and, therefore, lower enlisted basic pay for a member at a given year of service. In part, it also reflects a different incidence and use of S&I pay, as shown in Tables 3.1 and 3.2.

Table 3.4 shows average years of service at promotion to E-4, E-5, and E-6 by service branch for 1999. For comparison, it also shows average years to promotion for the Air Force in previous years, specifically 1990 and 1997. Time to E-5 is about two years greater in the Air Force than in the other services.

Average total pay also rises by YOS for Air Force officers whose commissioning source is academy or ROTC, starting at around $35,500 at YOS 1 and growing to $102,000 at YOS 30. Air Force officers fare less well than Army and Navy officers initially but do better in terms of average total pay later in their careers. At YOS 6, average total pay is $56,000 for Air Force officers and $58,000 for Army and Navy officers. The figure is significantly lower for the Marine Corps, $44,400, no doubt because the Marine Corps does not have medical officers in its ranks. At YOS 12, average total pay is $71,000 for Air Force officers, $75,600 for Navy officers, $67,000 for Marine Corps officers, and $68,800 for Army officers.

Table 3.4

Years of Service at Promotion to Each Grade, by Branch of Service

Grade	Army FY99	Navy FY99	Marine Corps FY99	Air Force FY99	Air Force FY97	Air Force FY90
E-4	2.0	2.2	2.5	2.8	2.8	2.8
E-5	4.6	5.0	4.2	7.2	7.5	6.9
E-6	8.9	11.0	9.0	14.6	13.7	12.1
O-3	5.5	7.5	5.8	5.3	4.8	5.2
O-4	10.6	11.3	11.9	11.1	11.5	12.0
O-5	16.5	16.2	7.7	16.9	7.2	16.4

SOURCE: Tabulation by Defense Manpower Data Center.

Air Force average total pay over a career varies little across broad occupational areas, as shown in Figure 3.5 for enlisted personnel and
Figure 3.6 for officers. (In the next section we discuss pay variation
that is due to special pays and bonuses.) Although S&I pays may be
targeted to specific occupational areas to ensure adequate flows of
personnel to the more senior positions, the first-order effect of this
targeting on average pay over a career appears to be small. In part,
the similarity in the average pay profiles across occupational areas
may reflect the broad definition of each area and the fact that each
area includes some diversity in occupational specialties. However,
the pay similarities remain even when we define occupations more
narrowly. For example, Figure 3.7 shows the average enlisted pay
profiles for information technology (IT) versus non-IT occupations in
the Air Force, where IT occupations are as defined by an OSD
commission on Information Technology/Information Assurance
Personnel. Again, the profiles are nearly identical. Therefore, any S&I
pay differences across these occupations are dominated by
similarities in other pay components, owing primarily to similarities
in the retention and grade mix at each YOS. For broad occupational

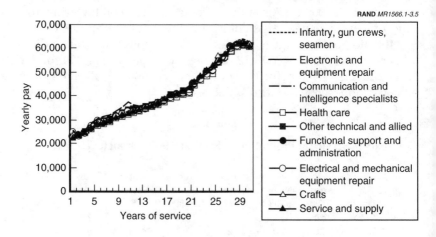

Figure 3.5—Air Force Average Enlisted Pay by Years of Service and
Occupational Area, 1999

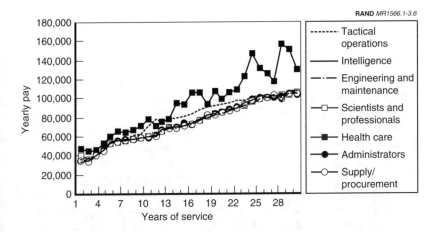

Figure 3.6—Air Force Average Officer Pay by Years of Service and Occupational Area, 1999

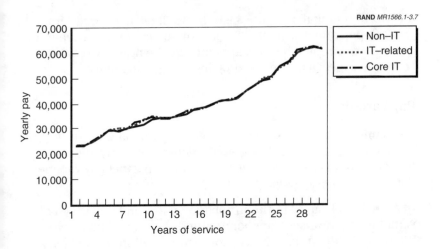

Figure 3.7—Air Force Average Enlisted Pay by Years of Service and IT Occupational Category, 1999

categories, Figure 3.8 shows the FY99 distribution of Air Force enlisted end strength across pay grades, and Figure 3.9 shows the distribution across YOS. The percentage of the force in each grade and the percentage in each YOS group are quite similar across occupational areas. These figures, together with the pay figures, point to a clear conclusion: *Differences in pay and retention by broad occupational area are quite small in the Air Force.* The figures suggest that S&I pays—although used—do not on the whole create much differentiation in pay. Furthermore, the similarity in the YOS and grade mix across broad occupational areas suggests that the Air Force provides members with similar career and pay opportunities regardless of occupational area. In contrast, the large size of average S&I pays for some Air Force occupations, such as pilots and medical officers, suggests that the Air Force has been able to achieve increases in pay for some occupations when necessary. Nonetheless, average total pay is dominated by average RMC, and average RMC varies relatively little across occupational areas. Thus, the differences in average total pay across occupations are dwarfed by the similarities in average RMC.

It is worth noting that Figure 3.9 indicates a relatively large group of enlisted personnel with 16–20 years of service in 1999. When this group flows through the 20-year point over the next few years, the Air Force can expect a noticeable drop in average experience.

Pay Variation

The similarity of average pay across occupational groups does not mean that there is no within-group variation. Similarly, the closeness of average pay across the services does not imply that pay variation is the same across the services.

In Asch, Hosek, and Martin (forthcoming), we find that much of the variation in pay arises from bonuses and special and incentive pays. We have divided military cash compensation into four categories: regular military compensation (RMC), special and incentive pays (S&I), bonuses, and miscellaneous allowances and COLAs. We analyze pay variation first with RMC, then successively widen the definition to include S&I, then bonuses, then miscellaneous allowances and COLAs. Our analysis uses data from the Joint Uniform services Pay System (JUMPS) for 1999.

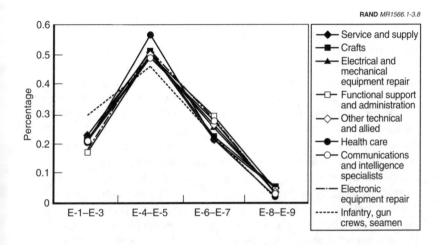

Figure 3.8—Distribution of Air Force Enlisted Personnel
by Pay Grade, 1999

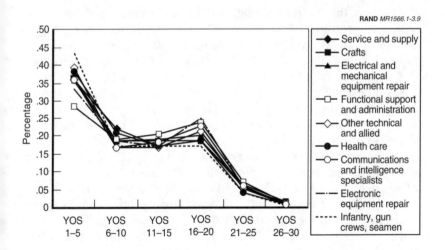

Figure 3.9—Distribution of Air Force Enlisted Personnel
by Years of Service, 1999

We find that the *range* of variation in annual military compensation for enlisted personnel in 1999 was about $10,000 at YOS 10. In part, this range reflects the fact that personnel are at different ranks; hence, at different pay grades. For instance, in the July 2001 basic pay table, the difference between an E-6 and an E-5 at 10 years of service is $2,174.10 – $1,962.90 = $211.20/month, or $2,534.40/year. After accounting for rank, most of the remaining difference in pay for personnel with 4–11 years of service comes from bonuses. As Table 3.3 shows, about 10 percent of airmen received selective reenlistment bonuses in 1999. The 10 percent was subdivided into 4 percent who received an initial award averaging $5,672 and 6 percent who received an anniversary payment averaging $1,293. In addition, 3 percent of enlisted personnel received proficiency pay, 3 percent received Flying Pay, and less than 1 percent received Toxic Fuels Duty Pay, Foreign Language Pay, High Altitude Low Opening Pay, etc. (see Table 3.1). Range, however, is not a good measure of variation because it does not account for the underlying distribution (more observations are massed near the mean and fewer at the extremes). For this reason, the *standard deviation* is superior.

For airmen, the standard deviation of RMC rises from under $1,000 at YOS 1 to around $1,500 at YOS 12. From there it rises rapidly to $4,000 at YOS 20. At YOS 24 it begins a rapid descent toward zero, falling below $1,000 by YOS 28. The rapid decline reflects the increasing homogeneity in rank of senior enlisted personnel; i.e., they are all E-8 or E-9. Similarly, the increase in variation over YOS 12–20 reflects an increasing diversity in pay grade as personnel are promoted at different speed and reach different ranks. When S&I pays are included, there is little additional variation. However, the inclusion of bonuses causes a substantial increase in variation during YOS 4–11. But from YOS 12 onward, additional pay variation comes from miscellaneous allowances and COLAs. These add about $750 to variation from YOS 12 to 27. As a rough gauge, the standard deviation of Air Force enlisted pay is in the $3,000–$5,000 range over most years of service, with about half due to bonuses during YOS 4–11, after which variation in RMC accounts for most of the variation.

Among officers, the standard deviation of RMC for the Air Force is nearly $8,000 in the first few years of commissioned service. It then declines to around $4,000 or less at YOS 3 and goes still lower in YOS 4–12. The amount of pay variation attributable to miscellaneous allowances and COLAs is minimal. However, the inclusion of S&I pays adds about $1,000 to the standard deviation of RMC alone, and the further addition of bonuses adds a great deal to pay variation. The major bonuses are Aviation Officer Continuation Pay, Medical Officer Retention Bonus, Additional Special Pay for Medical Officers, Incentive Specialty Pay for Medical Officers, Nuclear Officer Accession Bonus, Nuclear Officer Retention Bonus, Nuclear Career Annual Incentive Bonus, and Nuclear Qualified Officer Continuation Pay. Although only a small percentage of officers receive these bonuses, their large amounts significantly increase pay variation. Therefore, when examining the standard deviations of officer pay, it is worth remembering that much of the pay variation arises from bonuses that are received by a small proportion of officers. Around 3 percent of Army officers, 9 percent of Air Force officers, 7 percent of Marine Corps officers, and 13–14 percent of Navy officers receive these bonuses.

DISCUSSION

Civilian pay trends during the past five years have shown slow, steady growth in real wages and little change in wage dispersion within age/education groups. For example, for 22- to 26-year-old white males the wage difference between the median wage (50th percentile) and the 80th percentile wage was about $175 per week for those with high school only and those with some college. For 27- to 31-year-olds, the corresponding difference between the median and the 80th percentile wages was about $200 per week. For a 52-week work year, these differences translate to $9,100 for 22- to 26-year-olds and $10,400 for 27- to 31-year-olds. Again, these differences remained about the same from 1995 to 2000. Comparisons using other percentiles confirm the same point: little change in wage dispersion and steady wage growth, rather than an accelerating wage spike in 1999–2000 due to exceptionally low unemployment and exceptionally high economic growth.

We found a standard deviation of $3,000–$5,000 for airmen for most years of service. Bonuses were a major source of variation, especially in years 4–11. However, only 10 percent of airmen received SRBs, around 2 percent received an enlistment bonus, and several percent received proficiency pays of various kinds. Thus, skill- or proficiency-related pays play a role for a significant fraction of airmen, especially in years 4–11, suggesting some Air Force flexibility under the current system in recognizing differences in skill and proficiency. Nonetheless, for most airmen much of the variation in pay comes from differences in pay grade at a year of service.

Generally speaking, variation in civilian pay can be attributed to individual ability, motivation, education, occupation, and job. There are geographic differences in wages: When other factors are held constant, wages tend to be lower in the South, higher in Alaska, and higher in cities, for example. There are also risk-related differences in wages: Some jobs entail a high risk of injury or impairment (e.g., police, fire fighting, construction) or a health risk (e.g., dental hygienist, mining, work involving toxic substances). Nonetheless, much variation in private-sector wages derives from knowledge, skill, and ability, with knowledge and skill being the products of education, training, and experience.

The private sector does not need to promote high performers in order to reward them, and it is not shy about paying different skills differently. Moreover, even though each firm has a compensation schedule that presumably provides some internal equity, there is wide variation across firms. In contrast, the services operate under a single basic pay table, and promotion is a major source of pay increase. It is reasonable to suppose that promotion depends on ability, motivation, education, training, effort, and performance—the same factors that contribute to individual pay variation in the private sector. In addition, bonuses provide some "equalizing differences" by bringing military pay to a higher level relative to private-sector opportunities. Still, it is not surprising to find less pay variation in the military with its common pay table and limited use of bonuses and special pays. This finding, however, is "agnostic": We cannot say whether the military compensation system provides too little pay variation.

Chapter Four

COMPENSATION ALTERNATIVES

OVERVIEW OF ALTERNATIVES

In light of the Air Force's personnel situation, the civilian labor market trends that are adverse for the Air Force, and the small differences in pay across skill areas, it is useful to consider alternatives that could improve Air Force pay and create greater pay differentiation. We consider three alternatives.

- Alter the current compensation system by better measuring civilian pay, improving reenlistment bonuses, better recognizing hostile duty, and changing the pay table to better reward individuals who have demonstrated superior capability in their skill.

- Introduce a new pay component, *skill pay*, which would provide compensation for demonstrated skill attainment.

- Introduce *capability pay*, which would be based on current and future capability in the military, particularly leadership capability.

Before discussing these alternatives, we consider a different approach to improving the compensation that Air Force personnel receive over their military careers. That approach would be to raise the career pay of Air Force personnel by modifying the promotion system and specifically by reducing the length of time it takes to reach E-5.

Because promotion to E-5 takes roughly two years longer in the Air Force than in the other services, it seems likely that the Air Force could gain the support needed from the other services, Congress, and the Administration to speed up its promotion rate. Advancing promotion by two years would give Air Force personnel a significant pay raise. For instance, if an airman were an E-6 instead of an E-5 at YOS 10, his or her basic pay would increase by about $2,500. Faster promotion to E-5 would accumulate in higher pay over all subsequent years, increasing the present value of career pay. This could be expected to increase both first-term retention and retention at higher terms.

Speeding up promotions might require significant changes in Air Force personnel management, however. A job that today requires a new E-5 might be revised to require an E-5 with two years' experience in grade, and so forth. Promotion criteria would also need to be revised.

One drawback of speeding up promotions is that, if such an approach were applied uniformly to all specialties, pay would be increased even in specialties where no retention problems existed. Yet if retention shortfalls were widespread and were expected to persist, this inefficiency would probably be minor. Alternatively, the Air Force could consider speeding up promotions selectively. Promotions could be accelerated in specialties where the Air Force wants to increase career length or where outside wages are highest. As a result of selectively changing promotion speed, differences in rank would no longer reflect differences in military responsibility alone but would also reflect market opportunities. This would be a significant (and not necessarily welcome) departure from the long-time policy of providing equal promotion opportunity regardless of specialty.

ALTERING THE CURRENT COMPENSATION SYSTEM

The potential changes in the current system discussed in this section should be put in context. They represent modest changes to the current compensation system rather than aggressive changes to the components, levels, or structure of the current system. Furthermore, the changes are not exhaustive but instead form a feasible alternative to developing entirely new types of pay such as skill pay and capability pay. As the previous chapters make clear, the success of these changes should be judged in terms of the services' recruiting and retention outcomes. Thus, continued monitoring of recruiting and retention success is also important.

Measuring Civilian Pay Accurately

During the 1990s, the annual adjustment in basic pay equaled the lagged change in the Employment Cost Index (ECI), as prescribed by law. This version of the ECI measures how wage and salary costs change among private-sector establishments. Although the ECI measures overall wage and salary growth accurately, wage and salary growth can differ for different groups. In particular, the active-duty military force differs from the labor force at large by being younger and more educated, and the wages of younger, more educated workers tended to grow more rapidly than did the ECI in the 1990s. As a result, increases in basic pay fell short of increases in the market. And because the economic expansion lasted so long, these differences mounted from year to year. Therefore, although the ECI provides a useful starting point for considering how much to adjust basic pay, it is equally or more appropriate to check wage growth for the groups whose age and education are most comparable to those of military personnel. This can be done without legislative action. Detecting faster wage growth would naturally argue for a higher adjustment to basic pay.

Not looking at civilian wage growth relevant to military personnel runs the risk of misadjusting basic pay. However, tracking the wages of multiple groups leads to multiple estimates of wage growth. These must be considered jointly in deciding on guidance for adjustments to basic pay—a more complicated procedure than using a single index. Still, one benefit of detailed wage tracking is determining the extent to which military pay appears to be out of alignment with civilian pay by age, education, or occupational specialty. Such focused comparisons can be used in developing requests for bonus budgets or adjustments in special pays.

Thus, a case can be made for close monitoring of civilian wages accompanied by periodic, in-depth analysis that might require special surveys or the acquisition of special data. The process of tracking civilian wage opportunities would be greatly assisted if DoD arranged to link the personnel records of service members with their postservice earnings. The Internal Revenue Service offers the best potential source of information on postservice earnings, followed by the Social Security Administration. (IRS data are preferable because the SSA caps earnings subject to Social Security contributions.) But confidentiality considerations may ultimately preclude interagency cooperation. If so, perhaps the best recourse is a periodic DoD survey of veterans. The survey would have to be designed to sample certain veterans from certain military occupational areas at higher rates. A DoD survey could also ask about postservice training, education, employee benefits, and other items, and the survey could request permission to link a respondent's survey data to his or her military personnel record. This information would help illuminate what kind of jobs veterans took, in which occupations and industries, how much they were paid, how long it took them to find an initial position, and how frequently they changed jobs. It would also help identify what aspects of their military experience—training, teamwork, leadership, know-how gained from assignments and missions—proved most valuable.

Improving Reenlistment Bonuses

In hindsight, higher and more pervasive reenlistment bonuses might have reduced the decline in Air Force first- and second-term reenlistment rates. The Navy paid reenlistment bonuses in 1999 to 15 percent of its personnel, the Army to 11 percent, and the Air Force to 10 percent. The average bonus payments were $4,452 for the Navy, $1,949 for the Army, and $3,167 for the Air Force. The Navy's experience illustrates the feasibility of paying more and larger bonuses. The Navy's personnel leaders might be a useful source of information on whether the bonuses have hurt Navy culture or helped it.

To make reenlistment bonuses into a more effective tool for short-term response in the Air Force, there should be a prior understanding of the conditions that would trigger an increase in funds for bonuses *within* a fiscal year and an expectation that the funds would be made available. We understand that the services must fund additional bonus outlays from their own budgets and must first obtain permission from Congress to reallocate the funds. The notion that unexpectedly large reenlistment shortfalls can be tolerated for a year until new budget allocations are made, and that the new budgets will be sufficient to restore reenlistment, found limited support in the 1990s—until the dire conditions of 1999.

In principle, bonuses are a superb instrument for managing actual or impending shortfalls in reenlistment, particularly in response to temporary or cyclical variations in the factors that affect reenlistment in a particular occupational area. Because of persistent threats of shortage in some areas, bonuses tend to raise compensation in some specialties on a semipermanent basis; i.e., certain specialties tend to receive bonuses year after year. Given that bonuses provide an "equalizing differential" to make military pay more competitive with private-sector pay in these areas, it is to be expected that some of a year's bonus budget is in effect preprogrammed. Within a fiscal year, the opportunity for adjusting bonuses often entails a choice of reducing the presence or amount of a bonus in some specialties in order to introduce or raise them in others. There may also be little willingness on the part of the leadership to move money from nonpersonnel accounts.

Another concern is that making bonus amounts and bonus budgets highly responsive to manpower supply shortfalls might induce "gaming" behavior, with some members delaying their reenlistment decisions to see whether bonuses will rise. If so, tying reenlistment bonuses to expected personnel shortfalls could be problematic.

A greater worry is that bonuses will become too prominent a component of pay. From an airman's perspective, bonuses are temporary additions to pay for the duration of the current term. Their amount in the future is uncertain, and they do not count toward retirement benefits. But bonuses offer cash today, not deferred benefits, and many personnel do not stay for 20 years. In general, the present value of bonuses to the airman if they were counted toward retirement benefits depends on the airman's discount rate and probability of reaching retirement eligibility at 20 years of service. With personal discount rates typically 20 percent per year and higher (Warner and Pleeter, 2001), the present value of incremental additions to retirement benefits is small. Further, it is smaller than the present value of the cost to the government of financing the benefit on an accrual basis.

From the Air Force's perspective, the relationship of bonuses and retirement raises an issue of the optimal experience mix within a specialty area. Although it may be desirable to increase the average years of service, it may not be desirable to increase the proportion staying to 20 years or longer. The answer may vary from specialty to specialty, so the value to the Air Force of tying retirement benefits to bonus amounts would also vary by specialty.

Certainly, the bonus instrument could be made more responsive than it is today. Bonus amounts could be adjusted during the course of the enlistment term. For example, bonuses could be indexed to rise if the current bonus step rose above the level that prevailed at the time of reenlistment. This would result in higher bonus payments in areas where manning shortfalls are becoming more critical, and the higher payments should reduce within-term attrition (although such attrition is low after the first term). If personnel anticipated the indexing of their bonus payments, the expected value of staying in the military would increase, thereby improving future reenlistment rates. Moreover, uncertainty would be diminished if there were a stronger expectation that the bonus would continue into the next term, e.g., through an early commitment by the service.

Bonuses might also be modified to provide greater incentive for skill acquisition. In particular, the bonus anniversary payment could increase with skill level. Depending on how "skill" and "skill level" are defined, the role of bonuses could be expanded: They could be used not only to avoid manning shortfalls in an occupation but also to provide an incentive for skill acquisition during the term. Skill could be defined broadly to mean the skills and knowledge typically acquired within a narrowly defined (3-digit) occupational specialty, or it could be defined narrowly to mean the acquisition of particular skills and knowledge. The Air Force already designates skill levels within a narrowly defined occupation. Presumably, it would be possible to define skill steps between levels if existing levels (i.e., 1, 3, 5, 7) were thought to be too few. This would create possibilities for bonus payment increases *during* the term, and it would offer an additional degree of freedom in setting bonus amounts, which today depend on basic pay at the time of reenlistment. A bonus that accounts for skill level increases during the term might have the added advantage of increasing the reenlistment rate of high-aptitude high performers. In addition, Developing Aerospace Leaders (DAL) certification standards provide another indicator of skill, and bonuses could be structured to pay an amount dependent not only on basic pay at the time of reenlistment but also on a member's DAL certification.

Modifying reenlistment bonuses to reward skill and provide incentives for skill acquisition could also enable the Air Force to implement more-variable career lengths and YOS/grade mixes across skill areas. Such variability may be desirable when skill areas vary in the costs of recruiting and training, length of the learning curve, and value of experience to the organization. Reenlistment bonuses could be targeted to areas where longer careers are cost-effective. However, if the incentive were to remain in place and be stable in value, it might be better to consider a special pay rather than a bonus. The special pay could be "stepped" by year of service and grade.

However, using reenlistment bonuses or special pay in a way that results in more variable career lengths would require changes in the personnel management system and most likely in the Air Force culture, which seems to provide an implicit promise that careers will be quite similar regardless of skill.[1]

Reshaping the Basic Pay Table

Capability pay is designed to reward people for demonstrating superior leadership capability in their current and future jobs. It also provides an incentive for capable personnel to stay in service. But to some extent the same outcomes could be achieved by reshaping the basic pay table. It may seem paradoxical that the basic table can be used to reward capability: The table is common to all personnel, but not all personnel are highly capable. However, changes in the structure of the pay table and personnel management methods that provide greater incentives for capability may be feasible.

Incentives for increasing effort and retention and for sorting capable members into influential positions could be strengthened by restructuring the basic pay table to make pay grow increasingly rapidly with

---

[1]This is a generalization. An obvious exception is the management of Air Force pilots, where there are special pays (Aviation Career Incentive Pay, Aviation Officer Continuation Pay) as well as service commitments.

rank. Such a change would "skew" the table with respect to rank because each promotion would result in an increasingly larger pay increase. By creating nonlinearly higher rewards, skewness increases the incentives for effort and retention at any lower rank and, most important, maintains strong incentives as personnel move up through the ranks.[2] Highly capable members should benefit because, if they exert effort, they are likely to progress faster. In turn, this benefits the Air Force by ensuring a supply of highly capable members to high-ranking positions, where decisions can have greater consequences. A skewed pay structure is appropriate in an organization where the probability of promotion declines with each successive promotion (a pyramid-shaped hierarchy).

Microsimulation modeling of retention and productivity among Army enlisted personnel showed that increasing the skewness of the basic pay table increases effort incentives and the retention and sorting of high-ability personnel (Asch and Warner, 1994). The same model was used to analyze the components of the FY00 pay legislation and their effects on retention and productivity. The model predicted that the pay action would have a large positive effect on both retention and productivity (Asch and Hosek, 1999). This result is not surprising given that the legislation included pay table reform (which was subsequently implemented in July 2000). The reform gave pay raises to midcareer personnel in a way that generally rewarded promotion over longevity.

The microsimulation model showed that it is theoretically feasible to increase the capability of the military force through restructuring the pay table. While it is also possible to increase capability by raising basic pay across the board, the simulation modeling demonstrated that skewing is more cost-effective because it targets basic pay to higher-grade and therefore more-senior personnel, who are less numerous.

---

[2]To maintain effort incentives among midcareer personnel and to maintain retention incentives among the most capable officers and enlisted personnel, the reward to promotion should rise with rank. This is also necessary because there are fewer promotions to achieve in the future, as individuals ascend the ranks. To maintain incentives, the "contest prize" or promotion reward needs to increase with rank to offset the fact that there are fewer performance "contests" in which to participate.

The mechanism by which a restructured pay table would result in greater pay for capability is promotion, an event that may occur infrequently and depends on one's current rank and years of service. When promotions are infrequent, the discounted present value of the future higher pay associated with promotion is smaller. Therefore, the degree of pay skewness must increase when promotion speed is slow, in order to offset the effect of slow speed on expected future pay.

One disadvantage of relying on promotion to implement greater pay for capability is that promotion speed either may not vary much across skill or occupational areas or it may vary in a way that does not adequately reflect the differential demands for capability across occupational areas. Air Force culture puts a premium on providing individuals with equal promotion opportunity, regardless of occupation. If the pay table were restructured to become more skewed and, therefore, to reward and provide incentives for capability, the similarities in promotion speed across Air Force occupations will result in little differentiation in pay. Alternatively, varying promotion speeds across skill or occupational areas would differentiate pay.

Pros and Cons of Improving the Current System

The previous paragraphs discussed how the pay table and bonuses could be modified to strengthen incentives for retaining and motivating high-capability members, for acquiring skill, and for creating careers of different expected lengths. These changes seem compatible with the Air Force's culture of equal promotion opportunity regardless of occupation.

There are a number of reasons why pay policies to achieve these goals should build on the current compensation system rather than on entirely new types of pays or pay systems. Probably the most compelling is that the current system has been in place since the Hook Commission issued its report in 1948, and—while the system has been subject to some criticism—service members and policymakers have demonstrated enormous confidence in it by their reluctance to change it. It has stood the test of time, including the transition from a draft force to a volunteer one, from a post–World War II peacetime force to a wartime force during the Korean and Vietnam eras, and from a Cold War to a post–Cold War force. These forces have varied in size, personnel experience, skill, and aptitude. Nonetheless, the basic structure of the compensation system has changed relatively little, and there appears to be considerable consensus that the system has worked well enough, with a few occasional adjustments, throughout the past 50 years.

The Common Pay Table. One reason for the longevity and popularity of the current system, and why building on it by improving the current bonus system makes sense, is that the current system uses a common pay table for all personnel. It thus provides concrete evidence of the value of a common culture in the military, and it recognizes the equal value placed on patriotism and service, regardless of the member's particular skill area or branch of service. Furthermore, a common pay table helps make the compensation system transparent to the entire military community, including the reserve components, and makes changes clear and open. Movement through the pay table depends on promotion criteria that are also widely known, and a promotion process that, we think, is perceived by members as fair. The salary and merit systems used in the private sector are often much less transparent.[3]

A common pay table in which longevity increases are automatic and where promotions occur periodically and are based on demonstrated ability and achievement also has desirable features from an efficiency or cost-effectiveness standpoint. First, automatic longevity increases save the Department of Defense and the taxpayers the cost of conducting annual performance reviews for all military members. If the military moved to a merit-based system or a skill-based system that required periodic, perhaps annual, adjustments that could differ across small groups or even individuals, the cost of administering such a review system might be prohibitive. Administration of the system would require the time and effort of supervisors to provide input, Air Force coordination of the information, distribution of the information to salary review boards, meetings of salary review

---

[3]Because workers usually do not know others' salaries, they may believe, rightly or wrongly, that they are underpaid relative to their coworkers. Still, openness would not necessarily stop criticisms of a firm's compensation system. Workers might question why one group is paid more than another, or why certain workers should have merited promotion to a higher grade.

boards, and justification of the reviews to individual members.[4] Furthermore, once a significant part of an individual's annual pay adjustment fell under the jurisdiction of immediate supervisors and was not necessarily tied explicitly to easily measured or well-known benchmarks, individuals could take actions to influence the supervisor's assessment to ensure a positive assessment. Such "influence" activities would be in the organization's best interests if they resulted in improved performance on appropriate tasks, but would not be if they were intended only to make a person appear productive without any genuine increase in performance. In addition, individuals who were unhappy with their salary action might write letters to their congressional representatives complaining about the system, resulting in a perception that the system did not work, even when it did.

Currently, the promotion system provides a periodic performance review. However, promotions are generally viewed as a successful tool to pay members more and provide them with an incentive to work hard and attain the skills necessary to gain a promotion. The promotion system is not viewed as having excessive administration costs, given the value it provides in sorting and selecting personnel, and personnel do not seem to complain unduly about promotions. In large part, the perceived fairness of the promotion system rests on the fact that promotions are based on well-known criteria that all individuals have a relatively equal opportunity of meeting.

Another important fact to note about promotions: Despite the common pay table, pay can vary across individuals because of differences in promotion speed. Promotion speed operates to differentiate pay among individuals.

Arguments for Changing the System. There are also strong arguments against building on what some critics view as a flawed system. Although a common system—particularly a common pay table—has merits, it is criticized as a "one-size-fits-all" system that inhibits force management flexibility. Bonuses and other special and incentive pays create some pay differentiation among military personnel. In

---

[4]Not all promotions require centralized overview. For instance, enlisted promotions to lower grades can be made at the discretion of the local commander.

addition, they help prevent low retention and thereby tend to keep retention profiles more similar across occupations than they would otherwise be. The result is a high degree of consistency in the career length and experience mix of personnel across occupations. However, bonuses and special pays could be used to create more-varied career lengths and experience mixes. That is, an old tool could be used in a new way. Career lengths are also heavily influenced by basic pay and retirement benefits. We have discussed the potential advantages of adding skewness to the basic pay table, which might be thought of as a major modification to the table. A more radical change would be to alter the retirement system.

The Retirement System and Flexibility in Force Management. Arguably the biggest impediment to managing the force flexibly is the military's 20-year retirement system. Regardless of occupational area, the system tends to lock mid-career personnel in "golden handcuffs" until YOS 20 and gives them an incentive to leave at 20 years of service and begin collecting benefits. The services have come to accept the retention lock-in as a commitment that must be maintained to keep faith with successive cohorts of personnel. This can be viewed as an equilibrium situation. Service members are willing to commit to high retention given their beliefs about the stability of the compensation system, especially the commitment to retirement benefits. In addition, the services are willing to commit to sustaining the compensation system given their beliefs about how service members' retention and commitment to duty respond to it. Any move to deviate from the commitment threatens to destroy the current equilibrium. Any system will have flaws, and criticism of the current system is inevitably destabilizing if it is not accompanied by the presentation of positive alternatives for change. To gain acceptance, alternatives not only must hold promise of being superior when fully implemented but also require a transition plan that conserves the interests of incumbent personnel who otherwise would be affected by the scope of change or pace of transition.

That said, the role of compensation is so important in meeting national security manpower requirements that a periodic critical evaluation is in the nation's interest. Past studies, including most recently a report from the Defense Science Board, recommended restructuring the military retirement system. A restructured system would vest retired pay earlier—say, at YOS 10 or YOS 5—and the new retirement system would resemble a thrift savings plan, where both the member and the government contributed to the investment fund and the retirement benefit depended on the level and timing of contributions. These studies also recommended making the military compensation system more cost-effective by putting a larger fraction of military compensation into basic pay and other up-front forms of pay such as bonuses. Cost-effectiveness would be improved because service members, who on average are quite young, value pay that occurs earlier in their career far more than pay that comes in the form of retirement, whereas the cost to the government would not change as much. Pay actions, such as the FY00 legislation that offers a $30,000 bonus to members at YOS 15 who choose to stay until YOS 20 and retire under REDUX, and actions that increase basic pay and the role of bonuses, are policies that can help improve the overall cost-effectiveness of the military's compensation system.

Because of the current system's limitations, it is useful to contemplate other approaches to implementing greater pay differentiation in the Air Force while also addressing the Air Force's recruiting, retention, and pay issues. The next sections consider two alternatives: skill pay and capability pay.

SKILL PAY

Skill pay would provide remuneration for designated skills. Skill is not synonymous with occupation. A skill and an occupation might be the same, a skill might be present in several occupations, or it might be present among only some members of an occupation. To understand the prospective role of skill pay, we have found it useful to contrast skill pays with reenlistment bonuses. We have done this in Table 4.1. As the table suggests, a key rationale for skill pay is to protect a valuable stock of current and future human capital when replacing that stock is costly and time-consuming. This rationale contrasts with that of SRBs, whose purpose is to prevent or address shortages in the flow of personnel currently needed to meet manning requirements in certain specialties. The emergence of bonuses as the chief retention incentive had occurred by the mid-1970s, as bonuses supplanted proficiency pay.

It is instructive to review the history of proficiency pay, if only because "proficiency" sounds closely related to "skill."[5] The purpose of proficiency pay and its companion, special duty assignment pay, was to induce the retention of enlisted personnel who were "required to perform extremely demanding duties or duties demanding an unusual degree of responsibility," and to induce "qualified personnel to volunteer for such duties" (p. 477).

Proficiency pay resulted from the deliberations of the Defense Advisory Committee on Professional and Technical Compensation (also called the "Cordiner Committee"). In 1957 it recommended a change in the pay structure that would allow the promotion of a member to a higher pay grade without promotion to a higher rank. The Uniformed Services Pay Act of 1958 permitted the service secretaries "to choose such a 'proficiency pay grade' method for compensating members 'designated as . . . specially proficient in a military skill'" (p. 477). It also permitted the service secretaries alternatively to pay a flat rate of up to $150 per month as proficiency pay. They chose the latter method and never used the proficiency pay grade method; that is, the secretaries elected not to sever the connection between pay grade and rank.

Three types of proficiency pay were established: shortage specialty proficiency pay, special duty assignment proficiency pay, and superior performance proficiency pay. Shortage specialty proficiency pay was displaced by the SRB in 1975 and phased out rapidly. By 1977, only 7,000 personnel were receiving shortage specialty pay, compared with 135,000 in 1975. In 1982, the shortage specialty pay program was absorbed into the special duty assignment pay program. Superior performance proficiency pay was authorized until 1976 and then terminated. Special duty assignment proficiency pay was paid to "personnel performing such voluntary duties as recruiters, drill instructors, or reenlistment NCOs" (p. 478). In 1985,

---

[5]The source of this information is Military Compensation Background Papers (1996), pp. 477–481. Page references in the text are to this document.

Table 4.1

Features of Reenlistment Bonuses and Skill Pays

Feature	Reenlistment Bonus	Skill Pay
Rationale	Prevent manning shortages in critical specialties. Shortages occur when the flow of personnel in a specialty is too far below the current requirements for personnel in that specialty. Assessments of shortage are done by "zone"; i.e., by year of service range.	Prevent loss of critical skills, even if those skills are not used on current assignment and/or are not in short supply in critical specialties. Skill pay helps to conserve human capital that would be difficult, costly, or time-consuming to replace and is deemed vital to maintain the capability necessary to meet readiness requirements.
Amount	Bonus amount is the product of bonus step, basic pay, and term length. Bonus step ranges from 0.5 to 6.0 in increments of 0.5.	To be determined. The amount is presumably a function of the value of the skill to the service and the cost of replacing the skill in the short run and/or in the long run. The amount may also depend on the value of the skill in the private sector.
Duration and payment schedule	Payable over the term of service. The initial bonus payment is made at the time of signing the enlistment contract and typically equals 50 percent of the bonus amount. The remainder of the bonus is paid in annual installments on the anniversary date of signing.	To be determined. For example, skill pay could be a flat dollar amount per month or a percentage of basic pay. The percentage could rise as basic pay increased over a career. Duration of payment would depend both on the member's eligibility and on the service's determination that the skill should receive skill pay. For instance, at some future date the service might determine that the skill is no longer eligible. Also, the payment schedule could be designed to have an end point, e.g., YOS 20 or YOS 25, and a start point.

Table 4.1—continued

Feature	Reenlistment Bonus	Skill Pay
Eligibility	The member must be eligible to reenlist. The service must determine that the specialty is critical and has a current shortage.	The member must demonstrate that the skill has been obtained and maintained. The service must determine that the service's stock of the skill is critical to readiness and would be less than the desired stock if skill pay were not paid.
Adjustment	The service can change the bonus multiple at its discretion. Changes are typically not made more than quarterly.	To be determined. Skill pay would presumably be paid to all personnel possessing an eligible skill (not just to the personnel who reenlist at a given time). Adjustments would therefore affect all such personnel. Frequency of change in skill pay level would depend on a periodic assessment of the internal and external value of the skill and its replacement cost.
Harmonizing skill pay with other pays		Other pays include bonuses, proficiency pays, Aviation Career Incentive Pay, Career Sea Pay, and others. These pays affect the retention of personnel. It may be that personnel who possess an eligible skill are in specialties or assignments where retention is high. Payment of skill pay to these personnel would not be needed to protect the stock of skill but might nevertheless be made. Other personnel who possess an eligible skill may be in specialties or assignments where retention is low. Here, skill pay would help protect the stock of the skill. Targeting skill pay conditional on retention would lower the cost of skill pay.

Table 4.1—continued

Feature	Reenlistment Bonus	Skill Pay
Harmonizing skill pay with other pays		But targeting would make the receipt of skill pay, and its amount, more uncertain to the member, reducing its value as an incentive to obtain and maintain the skill. If skill pay were paid to all members with an eligible skill, it might be possible to reduce bonus amounts in some cases.
Stability over a career	The bonus is valid for the duration of the term. There are no guarantees that a bonus will be available at the next reenlistment point.	Presumably, skill pay would be highly stable over a career. The set of eligible skills would probably be stable over time. The payment schedule would be stable, e.g., a percentage of basic pay or a rising percentage of basic pay. And the end point of payment, e.g., YOS 25, would also be stable.
Flexibility	Bonuses are highly flexible. Bonus multiples can be changed frequently, and service members are aware of this.	Frequent or large changes would undercut the value of skill pay. But the service would ultimately have to retain flexibility to make changes. Rigid pay schedules would be inefficient in the long run if the need for a skill diminished. If payment level were maintained even though the need for the skill had decreased, members might come to view skill pay as unjustifiably inequitable.
Equity	On average, there is a high degree of horizontal equity in military pay. Given grade and year of service, bonuses create a fairly small difference in pay, e.g., $1,000–$3,000 per year among enlisted personnel. For most enlisted	Skill pay would create persistent differences in pay depending on a member's skills. The size of these differences would depend on the skill pay schedule, which remains to be determined. Small inequity already exists in military pay, and it is reasonable

Table 4.1—continued

Feature	Reenlistment Bonus	Skill Pay
Equity	personnel, this is less than 10 percent of their RMC. Officer pay is also highly equitable, granted an exception for special and incentive pays related to aviation and medicine.	to expect that small additional inequity would be acceptable if the reasons for it were well known and perceived to be valid. A large increase in persistent inequity could be cause for concern. Service members might doubt why, in times of war or during peacetime operations, their value to the service should be less than that of a member in a designated skill.

new proficiency pay authority limited such pay to special duty assignments. Special duty assignment pay was payable to members "when required to perform 'extremely difficult' duties or duties 'involving an unusual degree of responsibility in a military skill'" (p. 478). The word "proficiency" was dropped.

The history of proficiency pay suggests that much of the intent of the Cordiner Committee was lost along the way. The committee sought to create a pay for members who were "specially proficient in a given skill." In practice, proficiency pay served to increase retention in specialties with shortages—even though the shortages might be completely unrelated to a member's skill proficiency. Proficiency pay also compensated for particular assignments that, again, were not necessarily related to skill proficiency. Only superior performance proficiency pay seems closely related to the spirit of the Cordiner Committee's recommendation, in the sense that superior performance is a demonstration of proficiency.

In any case, it appears that neither proficiency pay nor bonuses had the purpose of conserving the stock of a particular skill. So skill pay represents a departure from the domain of both those pays.

Skill pay could enable the Air Force to give explicit recognition to the differing external market opportunities available to personnel in various skill areas. It could provide a means of explicitly rewarding and providing incentives for acquiring and maintaining skills that are essential for military readiness and difficult or costly to replace. Arguably, all skills are essential for military readiness, but some skills are particularly costly or time-consuming to replace. Because skill pay could vary across specialties or skill areas, it could create a means of varying career pay profiles across specialties or skill areas and thus result in different retention profiles and career lengths. Skill pay would be paid to those who have a given skill, even if they are not using that skill on their current assignment. The rationale for this approach is that it enables the Air Force to prevent the loss of critical skills and to maintain a ready inventory of the skill in case of loss of that skill or unexpected demand for it in the future.

Skill pay has some disadvantages. Once established, skill pay should be varied only gradually. Otherwise, pay would become less predictable for a given member, and the pay system could appear capricious. But problems can also arise if skill pay becomes too rigidly established. If changes in military technology and strategy bring changes in skill requirements, the skills covered by skill pay should change—but might not. Similarly, if the external civilian labor market shifts toward new skill areas, the ability of the Air Force to meet these shifts would be hampered by a system that defined too rigidly which skills qualify for skill pay.

Implementing skill pay would require that both the Air Force and Congress define how skill pay would operate. For instance, skill pay can be a flat amount per month regardless of rank and year of service, or a flat amount varying by rank and year of service, or a percentage increment to basic pay where the percentage might vary by rank or year of service. If it were implemented as a flat amount regardless of rank or YOS, skill pay would resemble proficiency pay or hazardous duty pay, such as Parachute Duty Pay. Those pays are a flat amount paid to compensate for the danger and skill associated with such duty, regardless of rank or experience.

There are two potential problems with defining skill pay as a single, flat amount. First, the value of the pay erodes over time with inflation. Although its value can be indexed (and Congress has implemented indexing for some military-related benefits, such as the Montgomery GI Bill), indexing is not currently used to maintain the value of S&I pays. Therefore, to ensure that the value of flat-rate skill pay is maintained, attention would need to be paid to indexing its value.

Second, an important goal of the military's compensation system is to provide incentives for individuals, especially high-quality personnel, to work hard and effectively. Currently, this goal is primarily achieved by means of promotion pay increases that exceed longevity increases in the basic pay table. For incentives to be maintained throughout a military career, it is critical that the pay be skewed with respect to grade. By *skewed*, we mean that the pay increase associated with promotion rises with each successive promotion so that, for example, the monetary reward for a promotion to E-9 exceeds that of a promotion to E-8. The problem with flat dollar amounts of pay is that they reduce the skewness of the pay system, thereby reducing the incentives for performance and productivity. Flat dollar amounts are a larger percentage of pay for individuals in lower ranks than for those in higher ranks. Thus, they flatten the pay system and reduce the relative rewards for higher promotion, dampening incentive. In contrast, skill pay that is a percentage increment to basic pay, where the percentage might rise by rank or year of service, could enhance incentive by increasing the degree of skewness and increasing the relative rewards to higher promotion.

The skill pay percentages could be designed to vary by skill group, so that different groups differed in their rewards for promotion versus experience versus time in grade; that is, skill pay could break the link between rank and grade.

Skill pay would create persistent differences in pay across members and would thus decrease pay equity. The military pay system has a high degree of pay equity, although there are pay differences due to special and incentive pays and allowances. Small increases in inequity probably would not be disturbing, especially if members understood the reasons for the change in pay structure. However, large increases in inequity might create tensions. Pay inequity is difficult to explain on the battlefield when everyone is at risk and performing as a team is crucial. That said, some difference in pay might be cost-effective in assuring that manning requirements are met; i.e., that the right mix of personnel reaches the battlefield.

In addition to specifying the skill pay table and determining the mechanism for adjusting skill pay, the implementation of skill pay would require defining which skills to reward, assuring the skills have been acquired and maintained, and determining if and when skill pay terminates. The amount of skill pay could be based on pass/fail certification or on criteria assessing the breadth and depth of skills and possibly proficiency in their use. Some of the implementation costs are set-up costs and periodic fixed costs, e.g., for reviewing the skill pay schedules and the criteria for selecting skills. Other costs are recurrent, for example, assurance of a service member's skill acquisition and maintenance.

CAPABILITY PAY

The Air Force must conserve the supply of personnel who have demonstrated their capacity for effective decisionmaking and leadership. Leadership is important in determining the effectiveness of an organization, and individuals differ in their leadership capability. Leaders in the highest ranks hold positions of greatest authority and responsibility; by implication the decisions made by high-ranking leaders can affect the efficiency and morale of all personnel under that authority. Timely, effective, cost-effective decisions have a direct bearing on military capability. Resources can be efficiently allocated to activities, or they can be misallocated—resulting in higher cost, lower output, and less capability. Good leadership can build cohesion, communicate objective and mission, and inspire personnel to peak performance. Weak leadership, even when cloaked in a "command profile" and stentorian voice, may result in wastage, lower performance, cynicism, the loss of personnel, and an unwillingness or lack of incentive to pass undistorted information from lower echelons to the top. These comments apply especially to officers, whose decisions can affect wide portions of the organization, and to senior enlisted personnel, whose role in accomplishing missions is equally vital.

The concept of capability pay, as we understand it, rests on the notion that personnel differ in their leadership capability. We assume that a person's leadership capability depends on skills, knowledge, and experience, which in turn depend on opportunities, incentives, effort, and aptitude. Although an organization cannot provide a person with talent for leadership, the organization can make people into better leaders by providing leadership training, relevant assignments, and incentives.

Capability pay is not implementable without an empirical basis for determining leadership capability. We do not have studies or evidence on the topic of what constitutes leadership capability, how it can be measured (e.g., in junior or midgrade officers and midcareer [E-5 and E-6] enlisted members), and how effectively such measures are put into practice. It is a difficult challenge to come up with objective criteria on what constitutes leadership capability, verify their accuracy and reliability, and provide assurance that they can be implemented without a heavy or excessive administrative burden. In some ways, the challenge is already being met through the process that determines who is promoted and who is selected for career-building assignments. What must be added to this process are the objective, implementable criteria for leadership capability.

A person's accumulation of skills, knowledge, and experiences relevant to positions of high responsibility—e.g., command positions— might be either a coincidental by-product of coming up through the ranks or the result of careful, planned personnel management. The Air Force's Developing Aerospace Leaders (DAL) initiative, for instance, represents a move toward careful planning. Further, an organization can provide incentives to induce personnel to pursue a path to develop their leadership capability. The incentives should induce high levels of effort and commitment and be at least strong enough to retain personnel in sufficient quantities to create an adequate-sized pool of future leader candidates. From these points it follows that developing leadership capability depends both on personnel management and on the structure of compensation.

Symptoms of concern about a system's capacity to create future leaders include a lack of breadth and depth of experience among personnel. For instance, personnel might not be assigned to the full set of assignments thought to provide the best preparation, and they might spend too little time on an assignment to learn it in detail. These symptoms are closely connected with the personnel management system. Two other symptoms are low retention (e.g., high loss rate of captains) and a lack of incentive to solve systemic problems (e.g., an officer may avoid actions because they could be disruptive in the short run, even though they may yield benefits after his assignment is over). These symptoms relate to the compensation system, including performance evaluation.

Capability pay would recognize superior individual capability—both current and prospective—presumably as revealed through current and past performance. Capability pay seems worth considering when the basic concern is either low retention of highly capable personnel, including future leaders, or inadequate incentive for effort. That is, stronger incentives to perform and increased retention rates are two reasons to introduce capability pay. Thus, capability pay would be based on performance, much like performance-based pay. By itself, capability pay will not directly solve problems related to a lack of breadth and depth of experience, which lie in the province of personnel management. But it could help in solving them by inducing personnel to select leadership tracks. Leadership tracks can point in various directions—e.g., being a general officer or holding high-level command positions in such fields as logistics, intelligence, acquisition, communications, or space. Thus, unlike performance-based pay, which directly links pay with current performance, capability pay also recognizes the potential for superior performance in the future.

When pay level is largely dictated by rank and year of service, as under the current pay system, there is no immediate reward for exceptional performance. Instead, the reward is deferred (future promotion) or indirect (e.g., selection for a prize assignment or location). As discussed earlier, the size of the reward must be larger if the reward is deferred (i.e., the degree of skewness must be larger), not only because the value of the reward is discounted but also because the probability of promotion to higher ranks is low. Offering capability pay is an alternative to restructuring the pay table: Capability pay could differentiate pay among individuals given their rank and year of service, and it could be structured to provide incentives for high performance throughout a service career.

Capability pay may also help retain high performers. These personnel form the pool of future leaders, and retaining and motivating personnel who perform exceptionally well today will confer a future benefit on the organization in the form of improved selectivity in choosing leaders. A large pool of well-qualified personnel increases the expected capability of the person chosen, reduces the chance of having to settle for a below-par selection, and increases the chance of finding a high-quality replacement if the original choice turns out to be below par. The assurance of having a well-qualified pool of leaders has enormous value because leaders make decisions affecting many tiers of the organization and numerous individuals in what can be life-threatening situations. This point is important in an organization like the Air Force, which has no lateral entry, because leaders cannot be hired off the street but must be selected from personnel in the lower tiers of the organization. Without lateral entry, personnel in those tiers must be capable of performing their current jobs and must have the potential to fill more-responsible, higher-ranking jobs in the future. For the Air Force to fill its leadership positions with well-qualified, high-performing individuals, it must hire them at the lowest ranks and retain and develop them over time within the organization.

The importance of retaining high performers in the Air Force makes the retention trends shown in Table 2.5 worrisome. Those trends suggest that the Air Force has been struggling to retain high performers in its enlisted force.

Mechanisms to Implement Capability Pay

There are various ways to implement capability pay. Design questions include:

- Over what range of grades and years of service would capability pay be payable?

- Would all personnel in the range receive some capability pay, or only a portion of personnel?

- How large would the pay be on average for each grade or YOS?

- How wide a variation in pay would exist, if any?

- Would capability pay be counted toward retirement?

- How often would personnel be evaluated?

- In what ways would the current performance evaluation systems for officers and enlisted personnel need to be modified?

The design choices affect the incentive structure created by capability pay, and the incentive structure affects the retention of personnel, their willingness to exert effort, and the extent to which highly capable high performers are sorted into positions of the greatest influence and responsibility. The latter will determine the transitional and steady-state cost of capability pay, as well as its harder-to-measure benefits. For purposes of discussion, we will describe a possible design for capability pay. In our view, however, it is too early to be confident that any given design is best.

Capability pay could be payable to officers after completion of their initial service obligation, around the sixth to eighth year of service. It could be payable to enlisted personnel after five years of service, which for most personnel is after the first reenlistment. From these starting years, capability pay could be payable over the remainder of one's service career. By delaying the start of capability pay to these points, its direct and administrative costs are reduced. In addition, it can be difficult to discern a service member's performance and potential during the first years of service because there is small scope for individual initiative. Furthermore, during the initial obligation, random factors may play a relatively large role in measures of performance, making it harder to extract a signal of the member's actual capability. Finally, the initial years of service can be a period of rapid learning for personnel. Officers who might begin their careers with less skill, knowledge, and experience, due to differences in, say, commissioning source, would have an opportunity to catch up during these years and would not be penalized if capability pay was payable only after the initial obligation.

With respect to whether all personnel in the "payable" range would receive capability pay, we distinguish between eligibility and amount of award. Although capability pay could be limited to the top third or top half of performers, we identify several problems with such a cutoff. First, some personnel will be misclassified; i.e., some high performers will be incorrectly cast as low performers and vice versa. Second, highly capable personnel who feel as though they can comfortably qualify for capability pay would have little incentive to improve their performance in order to qualify. Third, personnel who received no capability pay might infer they had poor career prospects and might consider leaving the service, even though capability pay was supposed to improve incentives and retention. Furthermore, the fact that some but not all personnel in a unit received capability pay might prove divisive, perhaps hurting morale and productivity.

Given the importance of equity as a factor in setting compensation, capability pay should be implemented in a way perceived as fair. "Fair" could mean that capability pay is spread among more individuals, or that only some individuals receive it but everyone is believed to have equal opportunity of receiving it.

As capability pay is spread over more personnel with a given budget, either the total cost rises or the average award declines. Moreover, even if capability pay were paid to all personnel, those receiving a low award could infer a negative signal and some might leave. On the other hand, personnel receiving a high award would presumably appreciate the pay and recognition.

There are different approaches to paying a capability award based on the service member's current performance. It could be a single annual award, in effect a bonus. It could be a pay increment over future years. Or it could be a larger amount paid over a shorter period. In addition, if the award were paid over the remaining years of service, it would be more valuable to those intending to remain in service longer. Also, the award structure could be designed such that for any given level of future performance, the size of the award was a function of one's previous awards. For instance, the award could be higher the higher the level of capability pay being received. This would have the effect of compounding the value of a capability pay award, because a higher award today would automatically lead to higher awards tomorrow, given tomorrow's performance level. Moreover, the structure of awards could be skewed so that as performance level rose, capability pay rose nonlinearly with performance.

In sum, the capability pay table could be two-dimensional, depending both on the current performance level and on the current level of capability pay, which in turn would reflect past performance levels. The table could be skewed in both directions, with disproportionately higher increases to higher current performance and to a higher level of capability pay from past performance.

This design has another possible advantage. It would enable pay differentiation among personnel at the same rank and year of service.

By implication, it would weaken the link between rank and pay, permitting pay to be higher for personnel who have a strong record of performance in their current grades. These personnel may be highly productive in their current grades and positions and may not want to strive for the very highest ranks. Equally important, a service may want to keep these personnel in their current grades and positions rather than be forced to promote them to increase their pay. Thus, capability pay becomes a means of rewarding officers for their leadership capability in areas requiring a high level of technical competence as opposed to their general leadership capability. This possible role for capability pay intersects with the role of skill pay. By the same token, however, capability pay might also be a means of extending the time an officer spent in a position (longer time on assignment) even though he or she was on a general officer track.

Modeling and empirical work are required to evaluate alternative structures for capability pay. The analysis would consider how retention, productivity, and cost varied across different structures. Through policy simulation of these effects, it would then be possible to see whether high-ability personnel were more likely to be retained longer under certain pay structures. It would also be valuable to conduct focus groups and surveys to learn whether officers and enlisted personnel would be receptive to capability pay and in what form.

Although capability pay has potential benefits, it also has significant administrative costs. As mentioned above, a working definition of "leadership capability" must first be determined. A person's performance would be evaluated periodically—say, annually—and ranked against the performance of others and/or against a standard with respect to leadership capability. In many positions, judgment and initiative are important, and of course personnel do not follow a regime of repetitive activities. Careful, subjective evaluation of performance is required. We assume the evaluation system would be built on that used in the promotion system. So it seems likely that performance would be assessed relative to that of peers. The evaluator would have to operate under guidance prohibiting awarding the highest rating too frequently. One way of constraining the evaluator is to assign a "point budget." This should cause the evaluator to return good relative rankings of personnel by their performance. There could be a separate point budget for each rank (or rank/year of service, etc.), thus allowing higher point assignments for higher-ranking personnel, for example. There also must be a mechanism for translating points into capability pay awards; the relationship might not be the same every year or across all occupational areas. Finally, if officers and enlisted personnel perceived the evaluations to have a large random component, the incentive effects of capability pay would be diminished.

Chapter Five

CONCLUDING THOUGHTS

In the preceding chapters, we presented evidence about the personnel difficulties facing the Air Force and discussed options for altering the structure of military compensation. The options included restructuring the basic pay table to make it more positively skewed with respect to rank, promoting personnel faster, paying higher bonuses, tying bonus payments to current skill level and current rank, and conditioning deployment pay on the number of previous episodes involving hostile duty. We also discussed skill pay and capability pay, describing the roles they could play and the issues involved in their implementation. In conclusion, we offer two points regarding approaches to evaluating possible new pays and the value of flexibility in managing the personnel force.

PATHWAYS FOR EVALUATING NEW PAYS

The effects and cost-effectiveness of skill pay and capability pay can be analyzed using microsimulation of individual retention and effort decisions in response to the incentive structure posed by the pays. Determining the schedules for skill pay and capability pay and the details of administering these pays would require close consultation with Air Force compensation officers. The simulation model would then be developed to reflect the features of specific options under consideration. Skill pay and capability pay probably would not emerge as highly flexible mechanisms for responding to supply problems caused by the business cycle. But they would be helpful tools for dealing with persistent, large differences between military and private-sector pay, and for encouraging high performers to stay in the service.

A complement to microsimulation modeling could be a demonstration experiment in which a subset of Air Force personnel would be randomly assigned to test or control groups, and the test groups would be offered alternative skill or capability pays. The retention behavior of each group would be tracked, or survey methods could be used to assess their reenlistment intentions at different points in time. Because of perceptions of inequity, such a demonstration experiment would need to ensure that expected compensation was equal across the control and test programs. There are precedents for the use of such experimentation methods in military personnel research. For example, experimentation was used to analyze the effects of newly structured educational benefits programs and enlistment bonus programs in the early 1980s. These experiments were extremely valuable in providing empirical evidence on the effects of different educational benefits and enlistment bonus payments and structures. Furthermore, this evidence laid the foundation for the adoption of the Montgomery GI Bill in 1984 and the expansion of the enlistment bonus program in 1985. Experimentation is a particularly valuable approach to assess a narrow set of feasible options for skill pay or capability pay.

Another useful approach to assess new pay alternatives is a survey with a "factorial" or "conjoint" design. Just as private firms often use survey methods to query potential consumers about their preferences and buying intentions with respect to new products or new product designs, the military has begun adopting such methods in the area of recruiting. For example, RAND is conducting a survey of American youth in the college market to ascertain their enlistment intention and interest levels under a variety of new recruiting policies targeted to the college market. The "factorial" or "conjoint" approach allows us to examine the effects of different policy factors on enlistment intentions and to determine which combination of factors leads to the highest enlistment intentions. Such survey methods enable inferences about how individuals might respond to new recruiting policies.

Similarly, these methods could be used to make inferences about the retention effects of skill pay and capability pay alternatives among

Air Force personnel in key skill areas. A survey could be designed that would target personnel in various Air Force occupational areas. The survey would include different alternatives for skill pay and capability pay. Analytical methods could then be used to discover which alternatives, or combination of alternatives, lead to the highest level of reenlistment intentions among each group. Surveys can be used to query Air Force personnel about their retention intentions under a large number of potential skill pay and capability pay alternatives. Consequently, the survey approach is a particularly valuable way to assess a large array of options in order to narrow down the field to a few feasible ones.

SECURING GREATER FLEXIBILITY IN SHAPING THE PERSONNEL FORCE

In designing alternatives, regardless of assessment method, it is important to recognize that long-term manning goals may be substantially different from the manning goals of the past. The services have begun to consider the potential advantages of longer careers in certain specialties and keeping personnel in certain positions for a longer time. In the past, the patterns of retention and therefore average years of service were largely similar across specialties. An increase in career length could take the form of increasing the average years of service, e.g., from 7–8 years to 10–12 years or more. It could also focus on keeping more personnel after 20 years of service and even extending the mandatory retirement date from 30 years of service to 35 or 40 years of service, again depending on the specialty and the position. Lateral entry could be expanded to bring in personnel at middle to high skill levels. Lateral entry might help avoid shortages and could introduce the latest skills and knowledge into the military from fast-changing fields. The counterpart to lateral entry is a greater use of outsourcing for tasks that can be done by private-sector contractors. More reliance on outsourcing would presumably have implications for service manning requirements and rank/experience mix. Skill pay and capability pay seem to have the potential for being effective mechanisms for supporting alternative manning structures and for gaining the flexibility needed to meet future manning goals.

FIRST-TERM REENLISTMENT RATES USING A
BROADER DEFINITION OF
HIGH PERFORMER

The following table broadens the definition of high-aptitude high performers to include AFQT Category IIIA (compare to Table 2.5).

Table A.1

**First-Term Reenlistment Rates for AFQT I-IIIA
Personnel Who Were Fast to E-4, and Others**

	1996	1997	1998	1999
Air Force				
AFQT I-IIIA Fast to E-4	41	49	46	41
Others	57	50	50	44
Army				
AFQT I-IIIA Fast to E-4	33	43	39	47
Others	45	51	47	42
Navy				
AFQT I-IIIA Fast to E-4	37	34	35	35
Others	30	29	35	32
Marine Corps				
AFQT I-IIIA Fast to E-4	26	26	26	25
Others	15	16	17	18

REFERENCES

Asch, Beth, James Hosek, Jeremy Arkes, C. Christine Fair, Jennifer Sharp, and Mark Totten, *Military Recruiting and Retention After the Fiscal Year 2000 Pay Raise*, RAND, MR-1532-OSD, 2002.

Asch, Beth, James Hosek, and Craig Martin, *A Look at Cash Compensation for Active Duty Military Personnel*, RAND, MR-1492-OSD, forthcoming.

Asch, Beth, James Hosek, and John Warner, *Analysis of Pay for Enlisted Personnel*, RAND, DB-344-OSD, 2001.

Asch, Beth, and James Hosek, *Military Compensation: Trends and Policy Options*, RAND, DB-273-OSD, 1999.

Asch, Beth, M. Rebecca Kilburn, and Jacob Klerman, *Attracting College-Bound Youth into the Military: Toward the Development of New Recruiting Policy Options*, RAND, MR-984-OSD, 1999.

Asch, Beth, and John Warner, *A Theory of Military Compensation and Personnel Management*, RAND, MR-439-OSD, 1994.

Buddin, Richard, Daniel Levy, Janet Hanley, and Donald Waldman, *Promotion Tempo and Enlisted Retention*, RAND, R-4135-FMP, 1992.

Daula, Thomas V., and D. Alton Smith, "Are High Quality Personnel Cost-Effective? The Role of Equipment Costs," *Social Science Quarterly*, Vol. 73, No. 2, June 1992, pp. 266–275.

Defense Science Board Task Force on Human Resources Strategy, Office of the Under Secretary of Defense for Acquisition, Technology, and Logistics, Washington DC, February 2000.

Hosek, James, and Jennifer Sharp, *Keeping Military Pay Competitive: The Outlook for Military Pay and Its Consequences*, RAND, IP-205, 2001.

Hosek, James, and Mark Totten, *Does Perstempo Hurt Reenlistment? The Effect of Long or Hostile Perstempo on Reenlistment*, RAND, MR-990-OSD, 1998.

Military Compensation Background Papers, Fifth Edition, Department of Defense, Office of the Secretary of Defense, U.S. Government Printing Office, Washington, DC, September 1996.

Murray, Michael, and Laurie McDonald, *Recent Recruiting Trends and Their Implications for Models of Enlistment Supply*, RAND, MR-847-OSD/A, 1999.

Orvis, Bruce R., Michael T. Childress, and J. Michael Polich, *Effect of Personnel Quality on the Performance of Patriot Air Defense System Operators*, RAND, R-3901-A, 1992.

Warner, John, and Saul Pleeter, "The Personal Discount Rate: Evidence from Military Downsizing Programs," *American Economic Review*, Vol. 91, No. 1, 2001, pp. 33–53.

Winkler, John D., Judith C. Fernandez, and J. Michael Polich, *Effect of Aptitude on the Performance of Army Communications Operators*, RAND, R-4143-A, 1992.